A Perilous Advantage

The Best of Natalie Clifford Barney
Translated by Anna Livia

A Perilous Advantage

The Best of Natalie Clifford Barney

Edited and translated by Anna Livia
With an Introduction by Karla Jay

"Being other than normal is a perilous advantage."
—Natalie Clifford Barney
Foreword to *Souvenirs Indiscrets*

New Victoria Publishers Inc.

Cover design Ginger Brown

Printed in the U.S. by McNaughton and Gunn

ISBN   0-9-34678-38-3 paper edition

ISBN 0-9-34678-45-6 hard cover edition

Library of Congress Cataloging-in-Publication Data

Barney, Natalie Clifford.
    A perilous advantage : the best of Natalie Clifford Barney /
edited and translated by Anna Livia ; with an introduction by Karla
Jay.
       p.   cm.
    Includes bibliographical references.
    ISBN 0-934678-45-6 (hard cover) : $19.95. -- ISBN 0-934678-38-3
(paper) : $10.95
    1. Barney, Natalie Clifford--Translations into English.
2. Authors, French--20th century--Biography. 3. Americans--France-
-Paris--Biography. 4. Lesbians--France--Paris--Biography.
I. Title.
PQ3939.B3P45 1992
848'.91409--dc20
    [B]   92-13831
                                                               CIP

Acknowledgments

I would like to take this opportunity to thank all those who helped in the production of this edited translation. I am particularly indebted to François Chapon of the Bibliothèque littéraire; Jacques Doucet in Paris for allowing me access to Natalie Barney's unpublished manuscripts and permission to publish the two extracts which appear here for the first time, as well as the quotations used in my article *The Trouble with Heroines;* Berthe Cleyrergue for providing the photographs which illustrate the text and for allowing me to interview her; Idit Bires for photographic assistance; Agnès Thèveniault for a wealth of information and for allowing me to see her collection of first editions; and, finally, Karla Jay for her help, advice, enthusiasm and support.

Contents

Contents

Introduction
by Karla Jay

"If I had one ambition it was to make my life itself into a poem."
— Natalie Clifford Barney

Natalie Barney's entire life seems to have been carved of some more dramatic material than most of us have or would choose to have. Barney came from the wealthiest circle of American industrialist families and eventually inherited over four million dollars. (Today, this would equal about a billion dollars.) After her birth on October 31, 1876 in Dayton, Ohio, she grew up in Cincinnati and then in Washington, D.C. and Bar Harbor in select social circles.

Her father, Albert Clifford Barney, lived off the proceeds of a railroad fortune, and her mother, Alice Pike Barney, was also an heiress. Her father was far less devoted to the family than Barney suggests in "Renée Vivien." He seems to have been a self-centered man who had no great interest in either his work or his family. He retired on the fortune made by his ancestors and tended to ignore his wife and two daughters unless they did something that offended his rigid social sensibilities, such as Natalie's lesbian love poems (*Some Portraits and Sonnets of Women*), which his wife had either naively or defiantly illustrated with portraits of some of Natalie's lovers. Then Albert would intervene and assert his patriarchal authority, but generally he was more interested in enjoying himself in London while the rest of his family chose Paris.

Natalie greatly preferred her mother. Alice was an accomplished portrait painter who had studied with Whistler, and she shaped her daughter's devotion to the arts. Though Barney suggests in her memoirs that she was almost obsessively in love with her mother, the images and almost the words for this emotion are borrowed from Proust. Here, for example, is how Barney remembers waiting up for her mother:

> Such was the feeling I had for my mother, and when she bent over my bed before she went out to a party, she seemed more beautiful than anything in my dreams; so, instead of going to sleep, I would stay awake, anxiously waiting for her return, for whenever she went away I was afraid something terrible might happen to her. (text p. 4)

In *Swann's Way*, Marcel's memories of his childhood good-night kiss seem remarkably similar:

> My sole consolation when I went upstairs for the night was that Mamma would come in and kiss me after I was in bed.... I reached the point of hoping that this good night which I loved so much would come as late as possible, so as to prolong the time of respite during which Mamma would not yet have appeared. (Proust 13-14)

Perhaps, Oedipal/Electra devotion to one's mother was a proper sentiment at the turn of the century, but certainly, in a book written for the French public, quite familiar with Proust's famous remembrance of childhood, Natalie's (re)construction of her own earlier years would strike a resonant chord. It might also make her forthcoming confession of lesbianism easier to understand for a public well-versed in Freud (even though, as we shall see, Barney considered herself to be "naturally unnatural"). By evoking a cultural icon of Oedipal obsession, she attempts to make even a hostile reader accept the fact that she "learned to love our neighbor" in ways the Bible doesn't address, and the reader is not surprised when young Natalie's adoration of her mother is transformed into crushes on her mother's models during Natalie's adolescence in Washington and Paris.

The only oddity that emerges in retrospect about Natalie's

childhood is that her adoring mother, who had both daughters educated by a French governess and then sent Natalie to a select boarding school, Les Ruches, never seems to have encouraged Natalie to go to college at a time when higher education was becoming popular for the daughters of the rich. Nor did it occur to Natalie to go, even though her best friend, Evalina Palmer, attended Bryn Mawr. We might assume that both mother and daughter shared a disdain for rigid and traditional academic endeavors, and both preferred to remain in Paris to pursue an artistic and romantic life.

Natalie was not altogether without educational aspirations. While living in Paris, she hired Charles Brun (called "B.C." in "Renée Vivien") to teach her Classical Greek and to tutor her in some of the finer points of French poetics. Later, Renée joined her in her studies. Few women knew Greek, and decades later, Virginia Woolf would call it the "secret language" of men, one from which women were generally excluded because they were not taught it. By choosing to study Greek, Natalie and Renée rejected traditional subjects reserved for women and entered immediately and directly into the private domain of men. Renée proved the more apt pupil of the two and by the end of her life, she had managed to translate Sappho's fragments and expand upon them several times.

Generally, Natalie seemed more interested in living lovers than dead languages. After some adolescent crushes, experimentation, and early relationships, she was smitten by Liane de Pougy, the most famous courtesan of the Belle Epoque. Natalie's determination to "rescue" Liane from the demimonde, even if Natalie had to marry a suitor, William Morrow (called "Freddy" in her memoir) in order to raise the capital to do so, shows an early inclination to play the knight in her relationships with other women. This proclivity helps explain why she was drawn to Renée Vivien, whom she felt she had to save from her obsession with death, and later to Romaine Brooks, whose unfortunate childhood left her with little love of social commerce. From an early age, Natalie seems to have been drawn to unsuitable lovers, each of whom was incompatible in a different way, each of whom was impossible for her to live with, each of whom would leave her longing for (and feeling free to pursue) other women.

Because Natalie saw herself as a page (a knight in training) rescuing damsels in distress, the women in question had to appear to be rather more innocent and helpless than they were in reality. Renée Vivien is depicted by her and also by her biographers as having had no physical relationships with women prior to her liaison with Natalie, despite her deep emotional attachment to Violet Shilleto. It is unclear whether or not there was any physical relationship between Renée and Violet. Natalie does omit Renée's involvement with Olive Custance ("Opale") as well as Renée's correspondence with a Turkish noblewoman in a harem. Barney was well aware of both affairs, particularly the latter since she and Renée stopped to visit this woman in Constantinople on their way to Lesbos in 1904. That Natalie was well aware of Renée's other relationships is revealed in the remark she makes to Renée after the latter has discovered the infidelity of Hélène, the Baroness von Zuylen de Nyevelt: "Really, Renée, do you have the right to be so indignant?" Well, Renée would have that right had she been faithful herself!

To admit that Renée Vivien was perfectly capable of having multiple affairs herself would ruin the tale of how Natalie tried but failed to rescue her from the grip of the ruthless and unattractive Baroness. Natalie tends to emphasize the Baroness's power and tries to turn the reader against her by alluding to her Semitic origins (the Baroness was one of the Rothchilds). Renée is depicted as a helpless pigeon in the grasp of a vulture, but Natalie fails to point out that Renée was the heiress to a dry goods fortune. Thus, she had no need of the Baroness's money and was just as capable of fleeing the Baroness as she was of suddenly ending her relationship with Natalie. By emphasizing the power of Hélène de Nyevelt, aided and abetted by a greedy governess, Natalie presents Renée as the helpless victim of irresistible forces— someone without the will or the strength to leave despite her clear preference for Natalie. In a revealing comment, Natalie confesses, "I was obsessed by her flight from me...." Natalie, as the page, saw herself as the one who loved and then moved on to other adventures. By breaking with Natalie, Renée had turned the tables on her in a painful way.

In death, Renée found the ultimate way to reject Natalie, who had remained in contact with her after the final breakup of their relationship. The cold finality of this end is emphasized by the rudeness of an unknown butler informing Natalie at the door, "Mademoiselle has just died." It seems highly improbable that a butler would make such a statement to a person of quality such as Natalie. He would be more likely to admit her to the house and let the priest or another person of her own social class break the tragic news. Here again, I think Barney borrows a bit from Proust, where little Marcel's written request for a kiss from his mother is completely and irreparably crushed by the unfeeling announcement of the servant Françoise, "There is no answer." (*Swann's Way*, 34).

While ostensibly and loudly mourning the loss of Renée, Natalie went ahead with plans to open her salon at 20 rue Jacob where she had moved shortly before Renée's death. There, she entertained the literary, artistic, and musical luminaries of the Western world for over fifty years, and her Friday "at home" conveniently brought the most talented and lovely women to her door; many of them, including Colette, Djuna Barnes, Lucie Delarue-Mardrus, Dolly Wilde (Oscar Wilde's niece), Nadine Wong, and probably Elisabeth de Gramont stayed in her bed as well. Men and women alike fell in love with her charm, charisma, and beauty (her white blond hair and piercing blue eyes struck all who met her).

Romaine Brooks lived nearby, and though she was involved with Natalie from before World War I, she remained somewhat socially aloof and watched the parade of Natalie's other lovers from a discreet distance. She, too, has been depicted by Natalie and her housekeeper, Berthe Cleyrergue, as amazingly faithful to Natalie, but Radclyffe Hall's letters, for example, indicate that Romaine was quite smitten with the author of *The Well of Loneliness*, though the latter found Romaine a bit too aggressive and masculine for her own tastes. Again, the forlorn, long-suffering Romaine may not have been as passive a victim of Natalie's infidelities as Natalie would lead us to believe. It is true, however, that

Barney's relationship with Janine Lahovary which began when Natalie was in her late seventies was the *coup de grâce* in their relationship, not so much because of Barney's infidelity but rather because of the intensity Romaine detected in Natalie's feelings for Janine. Romaine probably hadn't felt so threatened since Natalie had had a decade-long affair with Dolly Wilde. Romaine was not being paranoid, for Barney remained with Janine Lahovary until Natalie died in 1972.

Although Barney was drawn to Paris and remained there because of the intellectual climate of the city, she paradoxically adopted an anti-literary and anti-intellectual stance, an attitude which may have had as much to do with her American roots as with anything else. Although decrying the philistinism of her compatriots, Barney brought with her to Paris her native American pragmatism, which tends to view with suspicion any idea which is not immediately practicable.

As is evident in many of the selections, Barney viewed her literary output in an ironic light. One of her oft-repeated lines is: "My only books/Were women's looks." She frequently remarked that one should not write about romance, but live it. Elsewhere, she quipped that her favorite book was her checkbook.

Remarks such as these shed some light on her anti-academic stance. Barney obviously felt that ideas should be *lived,* not merely entertained. It was more important to be a humanitarian than a bibliophile. The attempt by Barney, along with Renée Vivien, to establish a neo-Sapphic creative community on Lesbos in 1904 and Barney's establishment of a literary salon for women in 1927 are examples of the urge they shared to convert theory into practice. (It is not far-fetched to suggest that Renée Vivien, darkly attracted to the *idea* of death, actualized the concept in her own quasi-suicidal end.)

Barney's writings contain many derogatory remarks about intellectuals who refuse to partake of the mundane or sensual aspects of life around them. In *The One Who Is Legion,* intellectuals are berated as "fraudulent usurpers of fame, mind-pickers and culture snobs." In *Critical Sallies,* she writes of "the English who pronounce the word art with a capital T" (125) and complains, "I do not understand those who spend hours at the theater watching scenes between people whom they would not listen to for five minutes in real life (125)." So strong a condemnation was also a reaction to the cultural snobbery of Europeans, as repugnant to Barney as the importance Americans placed on financial success.

This anti-intellectual stance was also part of a general rebellion against the literary and cultural situation Barney found herself in as a woman writer. Because she rejected the traditional male-dominated, Judaeo-Christian ethic in regard to religion and heterosexuality, she also rejected male definitions of literature as part of the culture she repudiated. In Renée Vivien's thinly disguised autobiographical novel about her affair with Natalie Barney, *A Woman Appeared to Me,* Vally (Barney's counterpart in the novel) remarks that the best way to write naturally is to make spelling mistakes. Vally goes on to note that there are so few women authors because they are forced to write like and about men. What Barney means here in part is that any writer who claimed serious critical attention had to remain well within the traditions and standards of style and context which male literary critics found congenial.

Barney clearly did not remain within those confines, and one of the results of her rupture with the male dictates of literary creation may have caused her to receive less acclaim from the literary establishment she so beautifully entertained in her home than she might otherwise have had. By refusing to conform, what Barney is attempting to do here is to (re)define the natural in literature, much as she re(de)fined so-called natural sexuality in her life and works. In a way that is perhaps unconscious, she unravels the patriarchal dictum that good writers should think and write like men. Instead of developing clear paragraphs and crafting well-developed plots and characters, Barney throws her ideas at the reader in a somewhat militantly non-linear, pseudo-random order. She replaces paragraphs with sentences that parade past one by one and stand so alone that they dare you to focus on one particular idea rather than on the others or the work as a whole, or even more rebelliously, to skip around in a way that would have driven your elementary school teacher into a tantrum.

Barney calls these one-sentence or one-fragment ideas her "scatterings" (the title of *Eparpillements*) or simply her *pensées* ("thoughts" or maxims)—a word that appears in the titles of two of her books. It is the latter term that was intended to provoke the male literary establishment, for the word *pensées* is typically associated with the seventeenth century writings of Blaise Pascal. Pascal, a French Jansenist scholar and writer, used the *pensée* to develop philosophical ideas about the nature of life, death, and an afterlife. Barney explodes the philosophical intent of the *pensée* by using the term for witty epigrams, *bons mots*, and perverse adages as well as for miniature tales and character sketches that are only a paragraph or two long. One source for these portraits is La Bruyère, whose witty character sketches livened the salons of the seventeenth century, but her most direct mentor in these endeavors is the witty, ebullient and irreverent Oscar Wilde, on whose lap she once sat and to whose lover (Lord Alfred Douglas), she was once engaged. She felt bound to these two men by a shared love of perverse witticisms that turn commonly accepted ideas, and by extension morality, on their heads. In a quip about lace-making, Barney focuses the attention on the hole instead of on the beautiful object. If we associate Barney's *pensées* with the dour Pascal, we too have been eyeing empty space instead of the fabric.

Her fragmentary style and her nonchalant approach to diction are the strength of Barney's "scatterings." The quick sharp wit of her plays and *pensées* is often based on the art of misquotation. The wit devolves from the unexpected twist she gives to what appears to begin as a familiar remark. Her observation on the sources of originality is a good example: "To mis-quote is the very foundation of original style. The success of most writers is almost entirely due to continuous and courageous abuse of familiar misquotation." There is a kind of Wildean perversity in her designation of misquotation as at once courageous and original. Like Wilde, she claimed for the epigram a significance belied by its apparent lightness: "The epigrams of today are the truths of tomorrow. The epigrammist has replaced the Oracle."

Her epigrams are characterized by style, wit, and a flair for the unexpected. Liane de Pougy praised Barney's epigrams as "exquisite, witty, and profound.... On each page she almost carelessly tosses a little masterpiece, written with humor and irony as fine as a dart..." (*Mes Cahiers bleus* 108, quote translated by Karla Jay). The description is a just one, and Barney's barbs make one laugh at the wound just inflicted.

Conventional grammar is often replaced with dashes and ellipses, for it is especially the latter, those three little clitoral dots, that typically omit the unspoken/unspeakable words of women's desire. The ellipsis, favored by Barney, Vivien, and Woolf, among others, was an often-used subversive tool of lesbian writers at the turn of the century, for it stresses that which is left out and unsaid in a world of legalistic male minds that want everything spelled out (and correctly, too). The ellipsis...yes, it may be the primary signifier of female desire that dare not speak its name, and Barney, one of its primary devotees.

But bold as her challenge to literary conventionality may have been, there was a side to Barney which was deeply conservative. Paradoxically, despite her denigration of intellectualism and her championship of spontaneity, she confined herself to a style and idiom more appropriate to an earlier era than her own, in a way which can only be termed "academic." In part, this choice was created by her worship of the French Symbolists (Baudelaire, Verlaine, Mallarmé) as primary literary influences. Since all of them had stopped writing by the time she began, it made her style seem conservative and rather outmoded. Therefore, one must ask why indeed Barney wrote in French, while most of her contemporary fellow expatriates for the most part wrote in their mother tongue.

As she recounts in "Renée Vivien," Barney had a French governess, who read aloud to her from Jules Verne and the *Bibliothèque rose*. Later, she attended Les Ruches in Fontainebleau. Obviously, one factor in Barney's choice of French as a language of expression was her bilingual education, a factor Barney liked to make light of: "Being bilingual," she remarked, "is like having a wife and a mistress. One can never be sure of either" (quoted in Grindea, 22).

Education in itself does not ultimately answer the question of choice of language. Barney had a deep love not only for French authors but also for the French language. She explained, half in jest, in her preface to *Some Portraits and Sonnets of Women* that the French language is more poetic than English, in part because English was more familiar and therefore seemed more pedestrian to her than her adopted language. She felt that she could have no poetic illusions about the words she had used since birth. As a further explanation, she offered the theory that her soul was inhabited by several departed French poets (one can only wonder which ones), and that was the reason her passion for the French language and for France was so strong. She hoped that one day the French would look upon her as one of their own authors (in the way that Joseph Conrad is viewed as an English rather than a Polish author, for example), but Barney remained a linguistic as well as a sexual outsider in the end.

Barney's audience has principally been French. Her first book of poems, *Some Portraits and Sonnets of Women,* though published in France, was soundly denounced by critics in the United States who saw in its Sapphic message a frightening visage of the libertine attitude they had always suspected the French of having. Barney tried writing under a masculine Greek pseudonym, "Tryphé," in imitation of one of her mentors, Pierre Loüys, who had pretended to be Bilitis, one of Sappho's followers. However, in Barney's case it concealed the vibrant lesbian message of her writing whereas for Loüys it simulated one.

As a result, her early writing alternated between French and English. She wrote poetry in both languages. Interestingly enough, her most personal work—especially her unpublished and privately published work—such as *The Woman Who Lives With Me* (the prose poem that she used to woo back Renée Vivien after their first rupture) was written in English. But the form she wrote in called for a French audience, for the French were used to reading epigrams and portraits whereas the genre had never succeeded in England beyond dinner party repartee or part of a play's dialogue. In addition, novels with lesbian content had a long history in France, and Barney was familiar with Théophile de Gautier's *Mlle de Maupin* as well as the lesbian characters in the work of such distinguished writers as Balzac and Zola whereas in the United States almost another century would pass before Dickinson was read as a lesbian!

The final factor in Barney's choice of French was her friendship with Rémy de Gourmont. Gourmont was a literary critic for the *Mercure de France* (a leading newspaper), and in a country in which people rarely agree on anything, Gourmont's writing was almost universally acclaimed, the Renaissance scope of his knowledge winning wide respect. When he became a recluse after being hideously disfigured by lupus, Barney was the only woman he would let in his home, and she alone could persuade him to venture out beyond his immediate neighborhood. Gourmont wrote two books—*Letters to the Amazon* (1914) and *Intimate Letters to the Amazon* (1927), in which he praised her as his muse and delight. By the time Barney published her own *Thoughts of an Amazon,* the French public was more than eager to hear from the lips of Gourmont's goddess. Americans, on the other hand, were mostly ignorant of Gourmont's work; therefore, his muse Barney was not translated into her native language.

Thus, it may be the case that the French people chose Barney as much as she embraced the French language. Yet the choice of French was fraught with literary danger which Barney herself was able to admit. She voiced her nontraditional themes in academic formalistic poems and plays in verse when most contemporary French writers considered these forms outmoded. Barney tended to imitate poetic forms that had been fashionable at a much earlier date. Colette noted about Vivien (but this was also true of Barney) that anachronisms in their writing came from having studied French literature relatively late in life. Like most people who have been transplanted into a culture not theirs by birth, French masterpieces struck Barney with a novelty that would be unlike the reaction of those familiar with them from childhood.

Barney's revolution, therefore, was not one of form but of content. First and foremost, she was blatantly gleeful about her lesbianism at least twenty years before Radclyffe Hall wrote the apologetic *Well of Loneliness* (1928). As early as 1901, she told her mother that she was "naturally unnatural," and later she came to view lesbianism as "a perilous advantage" rather than something to be ashamed of or contrite about. Certainly, by the time she wrote her "Illicit Love," she was well aware of the work of Havelock Ellis, of the early German homosexual rights movements, and perhaps of U.S. homophile organizations like One, Inc., the Mattachine Society, and the Daughters of Bilitis. But her defense of lesbianism goes well beyond the typical homophile plea for acceptance. As Amelia Lanier had done in *Eve's Apology in Defense of Women,* Barney rewrites Genesis to further her cause. She shows that God cursed heterosexuals as well as homosexuals in the Old Testament (actually, the O.T. Patriarch found He had made very few acceptable humans); after all, Adam and Eve, not Adam and Steve, were thrown out of the Garden of Eden.

In light of modern life and technology, it seemed prudent to Barney to review all of so-called ancient wisdom. The world, as she saw it, was overpopulated and paradoxically threatened at the same time with extinction due to the technology of the H-bomb that had so devastated Japan during World War II. In contrast, the nonreproductive love of lesbians (before turkey baster babies) seemed to her a safe and sane alternative to overpopulation, and her essay almost presages the reproductive freedom that women first experienced in the 1960s when the birth control pill was developed: When sexuality was finally severed from reproduction, it liberated gay people as well as nongay women. Lesboerotic love was totally harmless when compared to the destructive elements man had thought up. And as her scatterings clearly indicate, she associated war exclusively with men and felt that women had little to gain from either war or nationalism.[2]

I use the word *lesbian* advisedly here, for Barney felt no common cause with gay men, as her essay on Gide points out. Although she had a modicum of sympathy for the sad lot of Oscar Wilde as well as for her gay male friends and acquaintances, which included Cocteau, Gide, and Proust, she felt that their promiscuous, lustful ways were destructive sexual behavior whereas her own sexual adventures constituted a charming plan to make dozens of friends.

She also saw women as another oppressed group she was part of and needed to defend. In her unpublished memoirs, she declared that she had become a feminist after taking a childhood trip through Europe and seeing how poorly women were treated there. Like Zora Neale Hurston, she noted that women were the mules of the world. She saw that even women in power who are "the mistresses of slaves…[are] the slaves of the masters." And she knew that the financial power of men made a woman's relations with men an act of commerce, whether or not one was technically a prostitute. The best-developed example of her feminism in this collection is Barney's defense of breasts in the essay by the same name. It is superficially a reply to an attack on female anatomy by Ramon Gomez de la Serna. Barney, however, goes well beyond that by somewhat agreeing with misogynists that anatomy equals destiny, an ideal she subscribes to only in order to place primary erotic importance on women's breasts so that orgasm and pleasure are (re)centered in an organ denied to men. In a typical Barney twist, man is again God's poor first attempt of which woman is the perfected second try.

Barney's mockery of heterosexuals in general and men in particular is part of a broader attack on and dismissal of traditional values like marriage and religion, two of her favorite targets in her epigrams. She thought that original sin was not very original after all and hoped that all those "right-thinking" Christians could be replaced by people who think, presumably for themselves (115). She derided marriage as "a double defeat" because "it works on the lowest common denominator: neither of the ill-assorted pair gets what they want (110)."

Though Barney derided legal arrangements, she valued love and friendship quite highly. The portraits in this collection of Renée Vivien, Colette, Gertrude Stein, and Rémy de Gourmont attest to the warmth of her affection. Like La Bruyère, she believed that portraiture was a literary art form, again one that was not appreciated by her American compatriots. Still, she loved the form, and like many accomplished painters, she created several portraits of each model. Those found in *Adventures of the Mind* (1929) are quite formal and stylized images that highlight the intellectual accomplishments of each friend. The ones in this collection are from *Indiscreet Memoirs* (1960). By the time she had written it, all of these friends were dead, and she felt she could expand upon their private qualities in a way that would have been obtrusive had they still been alive. She believed that once someone was dead silence was the worst indiscretion: She had learned this all too well after Salomon Reinach had had the private papers of Renée Vivien sealed in the National Library in Paris in order to "protect" her reputation. Instead, his action helped push Vivien's poetry into obscurity. Barney sensed that the best way to keep these friends in the public eye was to celebrate their existence.

Not until twenty years after Natalie Barney's death has her work finally begun to appear in her native language. Now at last, we have Anna Livia's lively, accurate, and colloquial translation of Barney's version of her tempestuous affair with Renée Vivien, of Barney's witty sayings, portraits of her friends, and lesbian view of the world. Now at last, the women of the future for whom Barney wrote can become her newest friends.

Notes

1. I would like to thank the Scholarly Research Committee and the Summer Research Grant Program of Pace University as well as the Feminist Research Group for helping to make this work possible.

2. I have written at length about Barney's pacifism during World War I and Fascism during World War II in "The Amazon Was a Pacifist" in *Reweaving the Web of Life: Feminism and Nonviolence,* edited by Pam McAlister (New Society Publishers).

Bibliography

Grindea, Miron. "Combat with the Amazon of Letters." *Adam:International Review.* 29 No. 299 (1962), 5-24.

Jay, Karla. *The Amazon and the Page: Natalie Clifford Barney and Renée Vivien.* Bloomington: Indiana University Press, 1988.

Pougy, Liane de. *Mes cahiers bleus.* Paris: Plon, 1977.

Proust, Marcel. *Swann's Way.* Trans. C.K. Scott Moncrieff and Terence Kilmartin. 1913: rpt. New York: Vintage, 1989.

Apology:

May I be forgiven my coldness on account if its sincerity.
Ardour too can be cold.

✳

Why should I bother to explain myself to you who do not understand
—or to you who do?

✳

Quintessence? Mere leftovers…thoughts half thought.

✳

You only learn what you already know.

Readers May Choose Their Own Dedication:

At the beginning of this book I write your name in invisible ink
—your little name, which blooms.

✻

Despite myself I write for you; despite myself I erase you.

✻

For those who find their own thoughts here, before or after they
thought them.

✻

…Because you appear in it, and so does she, and she.

✻

For my beloved stranger, quickly lest I no longer dare.

✻

…So that certain pages may serve her as a corrective lens.

✻

Testament of abiding, though instant friendship.

✻

Do not try too hard to read between the lines, nor even between
the pages.

✻

…Whose eyes I love, and whose vision of the world.

✻

For my lady, whose lucidity is so much the rarer in that it is not
invariably, entirely vicious.

✻

…whose every word is an epigram.

✻

I venture to disturb you in the hope that I will please you.
…so that your long, myopic lashes will flutter against these pages.

*

…whom I have loved too well to be in love with still?

*

For he who became a priest, perhaps for time and peace to read.

*

For she who calls me "chaser of glow-worms."

*

Not for those who call me "Miss."

*

For those who call me "Natly."

*

For so many profiles, as they turn their backs.

*

For a mind high-brow with prudence.

*

For that more than upright citizen, bent backwards by his own importance.

*

For that other, bent so far forward toward others that he has never discovered his own balance.

*

And for she whose cautious little feet never risk a step for fear of falling.

*

For M…who views the world through her own vanity. For her we are no more than pocket mirrors.

*

I wrote this little book of epigrams for you, but others will read it more often.

*

For A, B, C…, all dead—alas how small the world is getting.

*

And for D, E, F, G, H, I, J, K, L, M, N, O, P, Q, R, S, T, U, V, W, X, Y, Z,
                —whom I would have forgotten.

Part One: Natalie and Renée Vivien,

a tempestous romance

A four year old Natalie in 1880

Natalie in Cincinnati

Interior of Natalie's house in rue Jacob

Natalie and René Vivien in the early 19

Natalie circa 1930

Natalie in front of the house in rue Jacob

Renée Vivien

Renée Vivien played an important role in my life, as, no doubt, did I in hers.

Born at the same time, she in England, I in the United States, from adolescence onward the same center of attraction drew us both. And that was Paris.

I spent my childhood in the outskirts of Cincinnati, running about with my playmates. Our French governess, being too heavy to follow, would sit under the great lime tree in our garden and wait for us to come back panting for breath. Once we were comfortably settled, she would read Jules Verne to us, or the books of the *Bibliothèque rose*. That was how my little sister and I learned French, in the company of our neighbors, Violette and Mary S.. It was they who were to introduce me to Renée Vivien, around the year 1900, when we were about twenty years old and all living in France.

But that was not my first trip to France.

Some years before the new century, my father, feeling that we needed a more serious course of study, had decided to take us to Europe. Being separated from our pets: two dogs, a bulldog and a blenheim, a goat, some baby alligators from Florida, a little parrot and a big one, made us more unhappy than saying goodbye to our friends. It was heartbreaking to leave behind my Shetland, Tricksy, that tiny, shaggy little pony which I used to drive in our pony-cart with my little sister, and which I was learning to ride, not without incident!

When we left Ohio we even missed the little river which, seen through a veil of tears, became unforgettable, like our house which had already sheltered the shy tenderness of first love.

The child who does not start off life in love with their mother, or their father, has been deprived of one of the most absolute of human emotions. Such was the feeling I had for my mother, and when she bent over my bed before she went out to a party, she seemed more beautiful than anything in my dreams; so, instead of going to sleep, I would stay awake, anxiously waiting for her return, for whenever she went away I was afraid something terrible might happen to her.

When she came home with my father, often very late at night, I would hear the rustling of her skirt as she passed my bedroom and tiptoe barefoot toward the ray of light which shone under her door. I could not pull myself away, though I trembled with cold and emotion, until she put out her lamp.

My father was known at his club as a *bon vivant*. Of medium height, well-dressed, his hair still blond, he was popular with women, who were misled by his assiduous attention. He cared only for his family, however. His affection for me was demonstrated with gifts and bruises: he would pull me back from the traffic with such vigor that I would have preferred the accident. In the streets of Cincinnati, trying to keep step with him, my attention would be seized by the painted wooden Indians which the tobacco shops used as publicity.

When we came home again safe and sound, Mother would scold us for having scared her, albeit unintentionally. She was by nature happy and self-sufficient; we worried her all too often and at times she would almost resent loving us. She hugged us only infrequently, moved by one of her rare surges of emotion. The desire to control and any feelings caused by mere habit, were foreign to her. Her motto was "Live and let live."

I consoled myself for being uprooted from my past with the thought that we were going away with Mother. But would I see her as often, could I watch over her as well as I did at home? What's more, my father had invited one of his two favorite nieces to come along.

But no sooner had we set off than childish gaiety took over, our tears changed to giggles at every strange novelty we encountered both on board ship and on the old continent. The shape of some of the hotel furniture and our first sight of a bidet sent us into fits of laughter. This latter, which I baptized the "French bath," is to this day a rare object in America, viewed with suspicion.

Before settling in France, we visited Belgium. Our parents, wanting to linger at their leisure in the Belgian museums whose horrific paintings scared us, entrusted us to a guide with instructions to take us to the Zoo. The animals there made us miss our pets. How indignant we were (this may have been in the Netherlands) to see a woman and a dog pulling a milk cart together while the man sauntered alongside, calmly smoking his pipe. From that day on we were feminists.

My apprehensions about my mother came true only too soon. I saw much less of her, for she preferred to go out with my big cousin. I accepted it as best I could since her sketch book, which she filled with drawings of all the people who captured her attention, seemed to make her happy, engrossed and full of life. Night after night we would laugh at the caricatures which distorted the figures and caught the tics and mannerisms of the hotel guests whom she watched closely at the *tables d'hôte*.

Unlike her usual, indulgent self, when she ran into old friends she would see them in a new way and would portray all their peculiarities. If travel broadens young minds, it is more likely to deform those who are no longer young...

Our cousin, dazzling and bedazzled, was fascinated by everything. Sometimes when there weren't enough beds, I would sleep with her. Since I was no longer in a position to watch for the ray of light under my mother's door, I turned my eyes and ears toward this blonde presence beside me and she began to interest me more than the surprises of the trip. I wondered a lot about the photograph of the young friend she kept hidden in her suitcase. Was he her fiance? Her future husband? I was filled with anxiety the night I saw her kiss the photograph before slipping into bed with me. My sense of impending unhappiness for her if she married the young man got confused with feelings of jealousy. But a good sleep dissolved these night fears and I woke up to see my cousin smiling again, already dressed and ready to greet me with a kiss as fresh as her seventeen-year-old *joie de vivre*.

So that they might travel unencumbered, our parents sent us

to Les Ruches, in Fontainebleau, as boarders—the same Les Ruches where *Olivia* had been a few years before. The atmosphere of feverish passion which permeates her little book no longer existed. The school had changed hands. I like to imagine that the grounds of that long red brick building, still visible from the road, have stayed as they were when we "little ones," used to play at croquet rather than "grand passion." Though there were torrid affairs, as in any boarding school.

We witnessed two small scandals. The first was caused by two of the "big girls," American sisters who imagined they were as free here as they had been back home. Flattered by the glances of two cavalry men on manoeuvres, they conducted a correspondence with the officers which was later intercepted. The second scandal affected us more directly. One of our classmates was the subject of great admiration because of her long braid of chestnut hair which would coil serpent-like beside her at night. Someone cut off her braid while she slept, but who? Was someone jealous of her? It was we who solved this mystery, but much later and in a most unexpected way.

In class we continued to learn cursive handwriting, drawing, singing, deportment and how to curtsey, dancing, horse-riding, composition and French poetry: La Fontaine, Victor Hugo and poems by Racine and Andre Chénier to learn by heart.

We also learned to love our neighbor, in the person of one of the "big girls." Her Greek beauty and all that poetry inspired me so much that I wanted to express myself in verse.

Before enrolling us at Les Ruches, my mother asked Carolus Duran to do my portrait. Not wanting any passing fashion to date this picture of me at ten, she dressed me as a page. This was, perhaps, imprudent for I continued to play the page with my beautiful schoolmate who encouraged my attentions by calling me sweetly, her "little husband." After a prize-giving ceremony in which she won the *Golden Bee* award, given to older pupils who had done brilliantly in their studies, she and I were separated.

My sister and I stayed at Les Ruches about eighteen months and then moved to our new house in Washington, which had been built according to a plan of my mother's. The city, designed

by a French architect, enchanted us with its squares and parks full
of magnolias where we could play, while the little negro children
invaded the waste ground and the empty lots for sale between the
houses. Sometimes an Italian with a barrel organ and a monkey
would pass by and all the children, black and white alike, would
gather round, attracted by the music. Swaying to the rhythm, tap-
ping their bare feet against the asphalt, the negro children would
begin to dance. All this took place under the watchful eye of Fraulein von N., our favorite school mistress from Les Ruches whom
our parents, at our insistence, had brought with us to America.
She was pleased by this arrangement too, because she would meet
up with her great friend, Mlle C., who was now governess to the
five daughters of the new Vice-President, our nearest neighbor.

I often went riding with my favorite of these sisters. Too big
for my Shetland pony, I rode a plump, capricious cob. We were
proud of our mounts, and of our riding habits. Drunk on freedom
and the balmy air, we would skirt the woods, now full of new
buds, which surround the capital.

One day, we caught sight of the most beautiful of the Washington belles at the end of one of the avenues, driving a phaeton
with a pair of horses which had won the latest horse races. At her
side was an attache from the British Embassy who had hopes of
marrying her. We galloped so quickly to catch up with her that
her horses bolted. When she had finally managed to bring them
back under control, she told us off in no uncertain terms instead
of admiring our skilled horsemanship as we had hoped. She was
lovelier still when she was angry. My companion had a crush on
the future Lady C., who was to become vicereine of India. She was
finally appeased by our excessive admiration, forgave us, and grati-
fied us with a smile.

When we were alone together once more, I told my companion about my own crush, whom I counted on seeing again over
the summer at Bar Harbour. My feeling for her was kept alive by
our letters, in which I assured her of my faithful devotion.

My mother hired a studio not far from our schoolroom where
the most interesting, or the most beautiful, women of Washington
society would sit for her. I would sometimes be present at these

sessions, perched at the edge of the platform on which the models
sat. One day one of these beauties, still tense from the ball the pre-
vious night, posed so badly that she begged me to soothe her
nerves by softly stroking the palms of her hands. This calmed her
down, so much so in fact that she relaxed into a half-doze, ruining
the pose. I began to caress her ankles, which were so slender I
could encircle them with my fingers. From there I would survey
her from head to toe, and, if she began to bend even slightly, it
was easy to call her to order. Using the art of touch in this way, I
learned not only to soothe my mother's headaches, but also to
calm my classmates nerves. How many hands were held out
toward my fingers, especially at exam time, though the healing
influence only worked on friends of my choosing!

My mother, adding architecture to the long list of her skills—
which she inherited from her father, (and he from his distant
ancestor, King Solomon, perhaps)—had just fitted out in Bar
Harbour the second of five houses she had had built.

One of the first nights we were there, when my sister and I
were settling into our new bedroom, we heard the dogs barking.
We got out of bed, and saw our Fraulein going down the main
staircase in her nightshirt and bare feet. In her hand was a pair of
scissors and as soon as she reached the vestibule, she began to cut
up Papa's boater as well as one belonging to an old friend of the
family who was staying with us at the time. He was transfixed
with fear at that bizarre sight. Once she'd finished her act of intri-
cate destruction, the sleep walker climbed back up the stairs with
haggard eyes and a heavy step, passing the landing where we
watched in horror, and returned to her room which was next to
ours. As we went back to our twin beds, we were convinced it was
she who had cut off our classmate's braid at Les Ruches, walking
in her sleep again.

After this revelation we fell into a light sleep. When the visitor
told them about the scene he had witnessed, our parents had no
choice but to let Fraulein go. As she waited to return home, she
even made an appearance at our neighbor's house. Alarmed by
this visit, we had to put one of the blenheim's collars on her ankle
and chain her to the foot of the bed. What anguish we felt when,

night after night, we would hear her take a few steps then, startled awake by the sudden jolt, go back to bed!

She was replaced by a handsome Austrian with beautiful manners, who hid her pale, tear-filled eyes from all but me. Comforted by my sympathy, she told me about her broken engagement to the son of a great Austrian family and how she had been sent away despite his love for her. Each time I saw her looking sad I would slip over to her and murmur kind words. As she seemed inconsolable and her black hair had begun to be threaded with white, I tenderly put my head on her shoulder and spoke to her in a low voice as though I were her lost fiance. The words I offered seemed to soothe her bruised heart, for she pressed me against her breast. I would go on talking, as though her fiance missed her and was loving her through me. Little by little she took heart and smiled her beautiful comforting smile once more.

At the end of the fall, since Mother and I were to set sail for Europe, we sadly said goodbye to each other but parted the closest of friends.

My mother had by now advanced from Carolus Duran to Whistler. So that she could take lessons with the latter, she rented rooms for us in a family *pension* called the "Villa des Dames" in the Rue Notre-Dame-des-Champs, on the corner of the Rue de la Grande-Chaumière where the Carlo Rossi School was situated.

In this *pension* next door to her painting classes, we lived in rather antiquated conditions surrounded by old wood panelling. The only bathroom was reached via a back staircase.

Mother had brought letters of introduction from her cousins in Washington but Whistler waved them away with a dismissive: "Who are all these ridiculous people?" Indeed, he needed no introduction to enjoy Mother's company. Every week after class, during which he would warn her not to try to be "too clever," he would come and take tea with her.

I am sorry now that I never met him for all I needed to do in order to see him was push open the door of the small sitting room. But instead I stayed shut up in my room writing letters— and God knows what letters! Later my mother was due to meet my father in London; he preferred that city to Paris where men take second place. Before she left, she entrusted me with a sum of money to be given to Whistler who had promised to do my portrait. But I never went to his house in the Rue du Bac to sit for him, and with good reason: when the opportunity presented itself, and even when it didn't, I spent all the money on flowers and presents for various ladies—and what ladies they were!

When I rode as far as the Avenue des Acacias in the Bois de Boulogne, accompanied by a relative or a would-be fiancé, superb creatures would drive past in victorias displaying their beauty. I was captivated by one of them, whose angelic slenderness singled her out from the others. My escort that day was the young hopeful who told me, to dampen my ardor, "That is Liane de Pougy. She is nothing but a courtesan."

I did not really understand what he was trying to say. Young American women of my generation knew very little of the demimonde, but I had no trouble imagining that this young woman was in danger. I even went as far as thinking that I would find it easier to save her if I married my fiancé, though I never actually did. But after I had sent her several letters and lots of flowers, Liane agreed to meet me and I ordered a page costume from Landof's in which to throw myself at her feet. As I went into her darkened boudoir, I saw a figure stretched out on a chaise-lounge. Moved by the sight, I had sunk down on one knee to offer her a bouquet of flowers when I heard someone laugh. Looking up I realized that the figure in front of me was not my idol but a stand-in and I got to my feet right away. A ravishing face with short curly hair like a Fra Angelico angel appeared from behind a curtain. Liane had hidden away so she could observe me... Seeing my embarrassed face she sprang forward, saying in her languid way, "Here I am." She was dressed from head to foot in diaphanous white. I was surprised to feel her white hand with its tapering fingers land on my shoulder with the weight of marble, and by how strong her grip was.

As she took her leave, Liane's confidante—whom she called Altesse—more experienced in affairs of intrigue than she, invited me to pay her a visit so that she could show me her studio in which stood the famous stained glass window she had had made, an allegory of the visit paid her by Napoleon III, her most renowned guest.

Liane's carriage was announced. She sat at her dressing table, I on a pouf at her feet. She contemplated me with a kindly, ambiguous look in her eyes as she retouched her lipstick and mascara, and suggested that I accompany her to the *Bois*. I was to sit at her feet in the carriage like a page so that no one would see me through the window. Then she took off her indoor gown, made of soft material rather like a monk's robe, sprayed herself with White Rose, adorned her neck and fingers with pearls and slipped into a town suit her maid had laid out, with matching hat, gloves and hand bag. I for my part had put my hair up and thrown my beige coat over my page costume. Liane swept me off toward the door declaring, "I already love your hair and the way your mind works," and we set off at a trot, drawn by two big white horses, toward the Path of Virtue.

What became of all that? A novel by Liane, the title, quite simply: *Idylle Sapphique [Sapphic Idyll]*. But one fine day my father found me in my bedroom reading a long letter from Liane. He was not pleased and brought me back to America where I stayed for two years, leading the life of polite society in more discreet company.

Even after I had come out I continued to send flowers, notes and poems to those I admired. Since I could only write blank verse, my old friend and confidante, Jules Cambon, then stationed in Washington, advised me to learn French prosody. During one of his leaves, when we were lucky enough to meet in Paris, he invited me to dinner at Fayot's so that he could introduce me to Professor B.C.

Despite our divergent interests—or maybe because of them—His Excellency observed my life with interest and pleasure, while I enjoyed watching him watching me, not from vanity but because he was a clear-sighted, warm-hearted, shrewd observer. If, in our literary conversations, he expressed a greater liking for Marivaux than I, it is because the wheeling and dealing of diplomacy also requires one to make "false confidences." As for "principles," as Philippe Berthelot was later to inform me, "One has only to lean

on them and they crumble!" That playful wit used to say, in that
voice which rapped out every syllable: "Everything works out—for
the worse!"

After those two years of society life, in which I played my role
as debutante very successfully throughout the series of parties,
balls, cotillions, luncheons for young ladies and Embassy dinners,
I was eager to resume my exploration of other worlds and, particularly, to pursue the kind of adventures which excited me, in contrast to the rigid protocol of high society.

My longing coincided with my mother's desire to return to her
artistic pursuits without fear of interruption. My father therefore
accompanied us to Paris and left us in a mansion which he had
rented for the winter on the corner of the Avenue Victor Hugo
and the Rue de Longchamp.

Once established in this house, which was equipped with a
sumptuous studio, my mother no longer depended on Whistler's
advice. He did not like to venture outside his old neighborhood
and replaced his visits with little notes assuring her of his faithful
admiration. His delicate handwriting looked like a water course
running in orderly lines between the wide margins of the page. As
for his physical appearance, I have only a pastel Mother drew of
him to still my remorse and soften my regrets. She probably did it
in London while she was renting his house, 'The White House' in
Tite Street, for the season. In this portrait he is wearing his mono-
cle, his eyes are sharp and blue, his hair and moustache black, a little blacker than nature intended.

While my mother was sketching models at the Académie Jul-
lian in the Rue de Berry, I was studying the complex art of classical verse with Professor B.C.

So that no one could interrupt us, we did not even let our society friends know we were there.

How surprised and delighted I was to meet two friends from
my childhood, Mary and especially Violette S., in the *Bois*. They
were living with their parents at 23 Avenue du Bois de Boulogne.
Maturity had done nothing but accentuate the grave softness of
Violette's dark eyes under her wide protuberant forehead and
Mary's blonde insipidity, which put me more than ever in mind

of one of Shakespeare's nonentities.

They immediately told me about their friend, Renée Vivien "who also wrote poetry" and who, like me, shunned company— she had just been presented at St. James Court—so that she could devote herself to her poetry.

I was to meet her at a matinee of the Théâtre Francais. The butler announced the arrival of the S's landau with my two friends and Renée Vivien and, at the same time, handed me an envelope upon which I recognized the handwriting of Liane de Pougy, then travelling in Portugal.

Preoccupied as I was, I only pretended to pay attention when I was introduced to the young woman who, at first sight, seemed charming but too ordinary to capture my interest. I was impatient to read Liane's letter.

I was no more attentive at the play (I cannot even remember what it was called) nor did I listen to my friends' chitchat during the first interval. By the second interval I could bear it no longer but took the envelope out of my bag and withdrew to the back of the box muttering apologies. By the glow of a night light I read this strange letter:

> For you who were my blonde sweetness, my Flossie, for you who were once, for you who should be and who are no longer, for you who were, inevitably, according to the law of nature by which all that is born must die. Even You and Me, and especially Us! …Your hair alone will never surrender, never be enslaved, a victorious rebel. It will ever be a pale moonbeam… growing still paler with time and yet more delicate, more capricious even unto the grave.
>
> I write you these wandering thoughts in memory of your hair, to bid it adieu…
>
> Yesterday the moon sulked and I went for a drive in the countryside by the gloomy banks of the Tage, drawn by five crazy little mules bedecked with ribbons. In front of me two young creatures were chatting and planning a happy future. Happy! Ah! …As though happiness were possible here on earth for those who know and understand… And I, I was sitting

behind them alone, isolated, and I turned my head so that I should not hear them. And I gazed off into the distance at the road we had travelled. The moon sulked, still hidden by the Milky Way, the White Way lit up the sky and I thought of you, Moonbeam, of your fine fair hair…

Yes, I thought of You, my little blue flower I will never see again, whose perfume intoxicated me oh so sweetly. And the trees rushed past so quickly. I felt as though I was still and the countryside was running past… Just like You, just like Me. Is it You who has gone away? … or Me? … or Us?

And a sweet sadness came over me, joyous and elating, making me part of You, my fair one, my Flossie… I was almost in tears.

Was it You? Was it Me? And my tears filled me with a pleasure more intense than the laughter and gaiety of the couple in front of me: the son of a king and his beloved. They would turn around from time to time, wanting me to share their joy.

"No, no, leave me to my dreams. I am happy as I am. Not alone, no, I am with one who knows and cherishes me!" And the road flew past! And I lowered my eyes to the ground. Then horror, disillusion!

I saw rocks and stones and mud, crushed, trampled grass, flowers covered with dust, manure, footprints, cart ruts…

…I wanted to hide myself in your hair but you passed by, pulling the petals off a flower, dropping them upon my eyelids and upon my forehead out of pity alone. My forehead will remain pure under the sweet-scented shower of pale leaves poured over me by your hand. And if they fade? Will you come back and scatter more? No flee! Walk on by! Fly away on your angel wings… And may no one snatch me from my torpor, from the sweetness of my dreams. My true beauty is safe and far away now from men's lust.

Written as my pen dictated and my thoughts flowed, for You, for Me, for what used to be Us.   — Liane

I was so absorbed in this evocation of my love affair that I paid no more attention to the last act. But as we left the theatre that frosty evening in early spring, my friends, anxious to put off the moment of parting, suggested a drive in the *Bois*. Violette kept rather quiet, except when encouraging her friend, whom she loved with an innocent and devoted friendship. She asked Renée to recite one of her poems, which she did very simply and articulately. From the very first verse she had captured my attention entirely.

Lassitude

Tonight I will sleep soundly and long.
Draw the heavy curtains round, keep the doors closed,
Do not let the sun penetrate these precincts.
Cast around my shoulders the evening drenched with rose.
Lay down those funereal flowers whose scent so haunts me
On the white cover of my deep pillow.
Lay them in my hands, on my heart, my forehead
Those pale flowers which seem like warm wax.

And I will murmur softly, "Nothing of me remains.
My soul is at last at rest. Have pity on it!
Let it rest in peace for all eternity."
Tonight I will sleep a death most beautiful.

I was taken by this sad poem haunted by the desire for death. Having failed in the mission I had set myself with such fervor, that of saving Liane de Pougy from a life I considered unworthy of her (and which she left in the end to marry a real Prince Charming, George Ghika), I took an interest in this young woman with such a gift for poetry.

How could I awaken her interest in life? In my life?

This is how she seemed to me as we continued to see each other: a young woman who was taller than me but bent forward politely so as not to seem so, a slim body with a charming face, straight mouse-colored hair[1], brown eyes often sparkling with

---

1. In the first of three portraits of Renée Vivien, Marcelle Tinay describes, with a lighter touch, "Her pale chestnut hair which still showed traces of the almost vanished childhood blond."

gaiety, but when she lowered her beautiful dark eyelids they
revealed more of her than was in her eyes: the soul and melancholy of the poet I admired in her; her shoulders stooped as
though already discouraged, her gestures a little clumsy, her hands
trembled at times, about to seize hold of something invisible
which had just escaped their reach. She usually wore sombre colors and her belt was forever slipping to the rear of her not very
curvaceous body, which lent a rather touching quality to her back.

Her sense of humor was easy to set off and she had a childlike
sense of fun which would suddenly halve her twenty years. Her
weak chin was particularly evident in profile; full-face no one
could resist the laughter of her full lips and her little teeth of
which not even the canines were pointed. When she became ani-
mated her smooth complexion, set off by a beauty spot, would
turn virginal pink.

If I describe her features in fine detail it is to provide a more
truthful portrait than Rodin's bust of the poetess now on display
in the Rue de Varenne Museum, which carries her name but not
her likeness.

Furthermore, I feel I know her better than she knew herself,
when she confesses:

> You understand me, I am a mediocre person,
> Neither good nor very bad, easy-going, a little sly
> I hate strong perfume and loud voices
> And grey is dearer to me than scarlet or ochre.

How, then, did she come by the poetic genius which inspired
her?

Genius did not appear to dwell in this young woman who
looked like so many others who, she used to say, were her kind
but not her kin.

I imagine that, as with Emily Bronte and Emily Dickinson, the
genius which visited or inhabited her, only took possession when
it chose.

Colette was also struck by the contrasts in Renée Vivien, by
her double nature, or split personality: the laughing young girl

and the poet in love with death. Judge for yourselves from the description Colette gives of Renée in *Ces Plaisirs [These Pleasures]*, toward the end of her short life:

> Since she lived such a short, reclusive life, my task (and most pleasant it is too), is to report that the young woman whose writing is permeated with despair was blonde, with dimples in her cheeks, a sweet laughing mouth and large soft eyes...
>
> I have about thirty letters from Renée Vivien. None explains the poet's secret melancholy... Each of these letters is like the others. Their childishness is easily explained; it is the same childlike quality which radiated from that charming face with its smooth, full cheeks, from that mouth whose lip curled delicately upward to reveal four little white teeth.
>
> Under a bush of hair, blonde, straight, fine, abundant, two chestnut colored eyes sparkled with gaiety and mischief. I never saw Renée Vivien sad. She would often exclaim with heavy aspiration after each of her dental consonants, "Oh my dear Coletthe, how disgusthing life is. I do hope I'll have finished with ith soon."
>
> No one took this impatience seriously, and none of her physical features reflected it, save Renée Vivien's long, long body, a body without substance, stooping forward a little, bearing her head and golden hair like a heavy poppy. She used to stretch out her long delicate hands, groping like a blind woman. I would tell her: "Renée, the only literary thing about you is your body." Her gowns covered her feet and she moved with an awkward grace, dropping her gloves, her parasol, losing her scarf or getting it caught on something...
>
> Two or three times in five years I caught her at work, propped up in the corner of the sofa scribbling on her knees. She got to her feet guiltily and apologized: "It's nothing. I'd just finished."
>
> Renée Vivien did not talk to me about her poems. If I persisted a companionable silence, a complete reserve about literary matters would change the subject. When she gave me a

book she would hide it under a bunch of violets, a basket of
fruit or a length of chinese silk. I will imitate her reserve by
passing over in silence the deep, tragic sadness which
characterizes her poems—at times beautiful, at others less so,
occasionally magnificent, uneven as human breath, as the path
of the wind, as the throbbing of a great ache, the poetry and the
short life of Renée Vivien.

Let us return to the period when we first met, when so many
happy possibilities were opening up before us. Our friends, the
S's, left for their villa in Nice, where we would be "very welcome."
We had scarcely bid them goodbye when Renée asked me to go
with her to the Palais de Glace (Ice Palace) where she wanted to
show me what a superb skater she was. I sat on the wall and
watched her figure skating, carefully keeping my eyes averted from
various professional beauties I had glimpsed previously at Liane's.
Not one succeeded in catching my eye which was fixed admiringly
on Renée's youthful silhouette flying toward me as though borne
on invisible wings.

One evening Renée invited me to her *pension* in the Rue Cre-
vaux. "To make it worthy of my coming" she had filled it with lilies, the flower she had dedicated to me:

One day you will fade, oh my lily!

Meanwhile, it was the lilies which were fading. There were
some crammed into the water jug and even on the bed. Their
whiteness lit up the dark corners of the room: it was dazzling, suffocating, transforming that rather ordinary room into a passionate,
virginal chapel, moving us to kneel—she before me, I before her.

I left at dawn; the snow, last innocence of winter, had disappeared but a light frost covered the ground. My white footprints
lay embedded in the white carpet between her street and mine.

A disquieting beginning in which two young women try to
find themselves through a mismatched love affair.

Renée's still dormant senses could hardly respond to my passion, her dawning love, fed and exalted by her imagination, took
over my role as poet-lover. After each meeting, "for the night was

to us as to others the day," I would receive flowers and poems from her. I have chosen the following fragment to bear witness to the beginnings of our strange love affair:

> You see, I am of the age when the maiden gives her hand
> To the man her weakness seeks out and fears
> And I have not chosen a travelling companion
> Because you appeared at a bend in the road.
> I felt the sweetness and the fear
> Of your first kiss on my silent lips
> I hear lyres break under your feet.
>
> With what kisses can I charm your languorous soul…
> What loving rhythms, what passionate poems
> are worthy to honour her whose beauty
> wears its Desire upon its forehead like a diadem?
>
> …Here is the night of love so long promised
> In the shadows I see you grow divinely pale.

Embarrassed by this excessive devotion, to which I would have preferred shared pleasures, I still loved the poems she sent me. Then I realised that this adoration, for which I was the pretext, was necessary to her, that she had found new inspiration through me, almost without knowing me. Love replaced the old themes of solitude and death—but love in a guise which few poets have celebrated since Sappho. I was surprised that she attached more importance to her writing than to her life, for if I had one ambition it was to make my life itself into a poem. I looked to life, I demanded of life the fullest expression of myself.

Writing detached prose or poetry, neither for nor about anyone, seemed to me an uninteresting literary exercise. So my first book, which had just come out, was aptly title *Quelques Portraits-Sonnets de femmes [Some Sonnet-Portraits of Women]*. It was illustrated by my mother, in complete innocence. News of this collection reached the ears of *Town Topics*, a magazine resembling *Aux Ecoutes [The Listening Post]* which published an article under the malicious title, *Sappho Sings in Washington*. What would they say, and what, moreover, would my family say if Liane's *Idylle Sapphique [Sapphic Idyll]* were published over there and the resemblance between me and "Flossie" came to light?

Renée Vivien had recently presented me with a whole notebook written in her neat schoolgirl script. Her writing had not yet achieved its later soaring heights. On the vellum cover, decorated with a lily and a lyre in rather doubtful taste, she had written: "For Natalie, and for her alone." Having read and re-read these poems, which I had inspired and which were far better than mine, I wanted to see them published. Renée however, aspiring to glory— she had a higher opinion of it than I—consented to let them come out on condition that only the name "R. Vivien" appear on the book. When this first collection was published by Alphonse Lemerre under that initial which could have stood for a boy's name, a young lecturer with a reputation for discovering and launching future geniuses, chose *Etudes et Préludes* as the subject of his talk and declared to the audience, "how one could feel that those passionate love poems were the work of a very young man in love with his first mistress."

There were grounds for the mistake:

Like a chimera you touch softly but do not hold me...
Your body is like a lightning bolt, leaving my hands empty...

Since this fundamental error formed the basis of his lecture, Renée and I had to rush out of the room, overcome with uncontrollable laughter. No one in the audience guessed the cause of our abrupt departure.

A few years later, when some other volumes of her poetry were published, she bravely signed them Renée Vivien.

A professor at the Louvre wrote admiringly about her and Charles Maurras in *L'Avenir de l'Intelligence* [The Future of Intelligence] devoted a long chapter of the volume entitled *Le Romantisme féminin [Feminine Romanticism]* to this young poet, as well as to three others: Lucie Delarue-Mardrus, the Countess de Noailles and Madame Henri de Régnier. Here are a few extracts from the fifteen pages in which he studies Renée Vivien's art, comparing it with that of Baudelaire:

>...But the amazing thing is that where Baudelaire gives the impression of an eloquent hoax, this young woman touches us by her sincerity. And she is a virtuoso.
>
>...The mere plaything of literary craftsmen becomes, in her hands, an instrument of joy and pain, springboard for deeply felt elegies or heart-rending tragedies. Of the 'strange dreams' which the poet shares with us, not one but seems to come from her personal experience!
>
>...The author of *Cendres et Poussières [Dust and Ashes]* looks set to outstrip her best models by the starkness of her lament and revolt.
>
>...Her motto should be: 'Modern feeling, Parnassian purity.'

As for her knowledge of Greek and her translation of Sappho:

>...Her intentions are mixed. She does not efface herself in her author. But neither does she efface the author.
>
>...If we take a look inside the *peplum*, drop the *chlamyde*, a modern woman appears, fully clothed, complete with ideas about Life, ideas about the World imparted to her by the old romantics. She is at her best when she leaves Lesbos and Sappho behind and translates herself.

My young poetess was beginning to be asked for interviews and appointments and, fearing the invasion of her privacy, she paid a governess to stand in for her, the most unpoetic looking woman imaginable. This woman passed herself off as Renée Vivien, discouraging further enthusiasm or pursuit.

Just after this first success she took me home with her to London where, in the famous Bodley Head bookshop, I found a copy of Sappho's fragments translated by Wharton. (No relation to my compatriot, Edith Wharton who would have shuddered with horror at the idea that there might be any confusion). This precious collection provided Renée with a basis for comparison with her French translation. She had it always by her bedside and it was the source of pagan inspiration of many of her future works. Desire alone does not a pagan make: I already perceived in her a christian soul ignorant of its own nature. While I was browsing through books at John Lane's bookshop-cum-publishing house, he recommended that I read *Opale*, a first poetry collection by a young poetess in Norfolk whose second collection he was about to publish.

I was taken by a number of these poems, so much so that I wrote an admiring letter to the author, sending her copies of *Etudes et Preludes* and *Quelques Portraits-Sonnets de femmes*. Opale responded with fervour:

> ...For I would dance to make you smile, and sing
> Of those who with some sweet mad sin have played,
> And how Love walks with delicate feet afraid
>
> Twixt maid and maid.

"Why don't we gather a group of poetesses around us, deriving inspiration from each other, as Sappho did on Mytilene?" I said to Renée.

She was so enthusiastic about the idea that we put it in motion right away by suggesting that Opale come back with us to Paris where we would be staying in a little hotel in the Rue Alphonse-de-Neuville, next door to the Rostands. My parents reluctantly let me do what I wished, but only after hiring as my chaperone a woman who had already filled that role before, in a *pension* where I'd stayed when passing through Paris. It was she, in fact, who had appeared as Renée Vivien to discourage the curious.

Kindly Professor B.C. was also sent to us to teach Renée Greek because she wanted to translate Sappho's fragments into French verse. After her lesson, he would correct a new book I was working on: *Cinq petits dialogues grecs [Five Short Greek Dialogues]*. I also used his learned, difficult calligraphy for a transcription of my *Lettres à une Connue [Letters to a Woman Known]* in which I recounted my affair with Liane. When I had finished this book, I took off the ring she had had made for me at Lalique's which was engraved round the inside:

"It pleases me greatly that you suffer in order to love and understand me."

This couple, in charge of our studies and our virtue, became lovers almost before our eyes. This had its funny side, for they were quite grotesque: he long and thin in a dusty frockcoat with a pince-nez which would never stay on his nose, and boney, ink-stained hands; she a hefty mare with the profile of an Aztec, wearing an enormous, and enormously ugly, beauty spot high up on her big hooked nose. These representatives of normality were unlikely to convert us.

Opale, enthralled by our plan, replied that nothing would suit her better than to join our group of poetesses. She told us that she would be coming to Paris in the spring with her mother and a neighbor from Norwich and that, in anticipation of the joy of meeting us, she had been inspired by the reproduction of my portrait as a page by Carolus Duran—which formed the frontpiece of my *Sonnets-Portraits de femmes.* She sent me this poem written in her large, cursive script:

> Her face is like the faces the Dreamer sometimes meets
> A face that Leonardo would have followed through
> the streets...

Renée spurred to join in, wrote me a sonnet in a similar vein:

> Your royal youth has the melancholy
> of the North where the fog washes out all colour;
> Discord, desire and tears intermingle in you,
> Grave as Hamlet, pale as Ophelia.
>
> You pass by, swept up in some beautiful folly:
> Strewing your path with songs and flowers, like Her,
> Hiding your pain behind your pride, like Him,
> But your ever-open eyes miss nothing.
>
> Smile, blonde beloved, and dream, sombre lover,
> Your double nature draws me like a double magnet
> And your flesh burns with the cold flame of a candle.
> My troubled heart falters when I see
> Your pensive princely brow and your blue maiden eye

Now one, then the other, then both at once.

I found this version more flattering than the role of frozen idol stuck upon some pedestal—later she would celebrate me, under the name of Atthis, in poems inspired by Sappho's fragments. Renée covered me in flowers and Lalique jewelry, composed more often of precious settings than of precious stones, in which crystal, ivory and enamel predominated. She made me wear them round my neck, my arms, my fingers and my ankles. There was also a strange comb on which a golden dragon vomitted a spray of opals across my hair.

She wrote two versions of our real-life novel. *Une femme m'apparut [A Woman Appeared to Me]*, influenced by the bad taste of our "belle époque," in which she seemed to me to have given in to the worst excesses of "art nouveau."

Being a poet, she has little of the art of the novelist, is unable to breathe life into either of her heroines.

The first version, *Vally*, was written while we were not speaking; the second when she had restored to me the name of "Lorely."

Vally and Lorely have the same "undulating" body and eyes like "iced water under hair of moonlight." The author clearly wanted to create a magical impression, but magic turned down the invitation and was replaced by the absurd. To exemplify this sad assertion, I submit the following detail, from the description of a decor she must have found bewitching: "A dried snake wrapped itself round a vase of fading black irises." While, "dressed in a white gown which both veiled and revealed me, I pulled the leaves off an orchid and unthreaded a chain of opals..."

I had to scold Renée for the first of these forced "femmes fatales" who resembled me for, in her second novel, she has me say, in the guise of her unlikely heroine: "In truth, each person comes to resemble the picture we stubbornly make of them: be careful lest you render me incomprehensible because you do not understand me." In one of her books she declares me "incapable of loving"—I, who have been capable of nothing else! Contrasting my love of love with her love of death, Renée believes I suffered from 19th century "spleen" in sudden fits only, whereas she made it the leitmotif of her life and art.

That she wanted to lose herself so entirely in suffering tells me how necessary it must have been to her poetic inspiration.

Despite the false mysticism which seemed to haunt her, in a sudden moment of lucidity, she recognised my restful pagan soul. In *Une femme m'apparut* she relates how I asked her a few days before Christmas: "What is this Christmas celebration? Does it commemorate the birth or the death of Christ?" If exaggeration there must be, I prefer that to other distortions.

When I re-read those two novels, I get the unpleasant feeling of having posed for a bad portrait artist.

I still wonder how such a poet could have written such prose. On the other hand, I cannot help but admire certain passages which sincerely express Renée Vivien's ruling sentiments. Here is how she describes our first meeting:

> I recall the now distant moment when I saw her for the first time, and the thrill which went through me when my eyes met hers of mortal steel, those eyes sharp and blue as a blade. I had the strange feeling that this woman was telling me my destiny, that her face was the formidable face of my future.
>
> On winter evenings we set off together for the Bois. My eyes were dazzled by the snow. All that brilliance seemed like the flowering of an imaginary wedding. Around and inside us was a nuptial chastity, a pure and sensual pleasure.
>
> I spoke to her very softly, in a voice made faint by the fears of first love: "You are not like Her whom I have dreamed about and yet I find in you the incarnation of my deepest desires. You are less beautiful and more strange than my dream. I love you and I know already that you will never love me. You are the suffering which makes one scornful of joy. I saw you today for the first time and I am the shadow of your shadow."
>
> Vally murmured, "I am afraid to understand you and I fear to draw you irreparably toward me... I would so much like to love you," she repeated.
>
> "My love is strong enough to stand alone," I replied. "I love

you, and that is sufficient for my rapture and my tears. You will never love me, Vally, for you have within you such a passion for life and sensation that all the love in the world would not satisfy you."

But Vally's ardour was infinitely pure, her desire infinitely chaste. "I do not know how to put limits on my body or my soul," she said, "since my body has a soul, and my soul a body."

I saw everything filtered through the smoke of incense and aromatic herbs. My strange happiness filled my soul with mystic wonder. Later on I realised that these were the Unforgettable Hours of memory and regret.

Though I regretted throwing such a soul into disarray, and being the unwitting cause of a despair which was distilled in her poetry into "pure sobs," I did not feel responsible for it. I did not want it to be like that, rather that she should love me "just enough to bring the sunshine into her life."

Despite all her fantasies and perversity, did not my presence often bring a ray of warmth and sympathy, rather than the baleful, lunar influence she described? The most surprising thing about me is, perhaps, how natural I am.

It is difficult for complicated creatures to get on well with those who are at one with themselves. We must, however, accept the evidence of other people's impressions.

Pierre Benoit described the unreal atmosphere which surrounds me. If my house seems as mysterious as Psyche's, that is because we discuss neither national events nor domestic problems.

This is how it appeared to that well known novelist:

> I know a garden, Eriphile, with rotundas
> Dimly lit by pallid domes...
> The shadowy domain of mystery lovers,
> Pale phantoms, youthful, charming...

(One might be excused for mistaking it for some bad Renée Vivien!)

I am told that after he visited me at the Rue Jacob with one of his friends, his healthy reaction was to regain his self-composure "by downing a glass of house red at the counter of a neighbour-hood bar."

Renée had, meanwhile, found her true voice, her strength, the right note for real poetry, having moved toward a greater simplic-ity, guided by the resistance of the verses themselves.

Free from the old extravagance, I would now only wear the flowers she sent me—from Parisian florists who were an integral part of our lives: all our notes to each other were accompanied by flowers. We also sent a precious bouquet of orchids in an irrides-cent Lalique vase to the Pierre Loüys, to thank them for their kindness, and for two deluxe volumes of the *Chansons de Bilitis* *[Songs of Bilitis]* which the author had sent us, dedicated in violet ink, in his beautiful handwriting which looked like a bunch of irises: "For Renée Vivien, this line of Keats: 'Forever wilt thou love, and she be fair!' For N.C.B. young woman of the future, her admirer, Pierre Loüys." In his thank you note for the orchids he told us how much Louise de Heredia-Loüys liked these flowers, adding that they had escaped a flower's usual destiny by being eaten by their cat, a ravenous gourmet.

After our next dinner at their apartment on the Boulevard Malesherbes, Madame Pierre Loüys took me aside and begged me to persuade Pierre Loüys to stop writing under a chandelier as the light was ruining his eyes. I decided to send him an excellent desk lamp made in America next time I was back in the States, which would be fairly soon as I had promised my parents to spend the summer with them in Bar Harbour. While I was there I learned to my surprise and regret that this woman, so concerned for her hus-band's welfare, had left Pierre Loüys for their best friend, Gilbert de Voisins. Since my *Cinq petits dialogues grecs* had appeared in *La Plume [The Quill]* thanks to Pierre Loüys, I dedicated them to him, with this echo, "To Pierre Loüys from a young woman of the future." We remained firm friends till the end of his life, which closed into total darkness under a sky deprived of light by the war.

But to return to the luminous Paris of peace time—Opale announced that she would be staying for a month in a residential hotel in the Rue de Chateaubriand which her mother had rented. Her first social visit was to us and I was enchanted, for when I clasped this fresh young woman, with her dazzling complexion, vibrating with poetry, I felt like I was embracing the English countryside. Although Renée spoke admiringly of her poetry, she remained reserved. After Opale left, having invited us to tea a few days later, Renée declared, "I'm not going." I asked her why. She explained that since she hated the world and especially her compatriots, she would not make an exception for Opale whose appearance and gay demeanour she considered unworthy of her poetry. Would she have changed her mind? Probably, for, sensing deeper motives for antagonism beneath her admiration and refusal, I reminded her that we must pass over the little defects and infelicities of the poetesses who were to be part of our group. To combat more effectively what I deemed to be the cause of her resentment, I pointed out that Sappho was more welcoming toward the women who came from far away to join her and, to avoid upsetting the harmony of their union, she tolerated even those of whom she was jealous, deriving inspiration from them. As an example I quoted, "You hate the thought of me, Atthis, you flee toward Andromeda." And didn't she remain attached to the unfaithful Atthis when she herself fell for someone else, declaring: "My feelings remain unchanged toward you, my beauties." Had I not convinced Renée by this subterfuge that nothing and no one could separate us? I do not know, for that very evening she received a telegram from Violette who was unable to leave Nice having fallen into a strange decline and was calling for Renée at her bedside. Renée went immediately to be with her, leaving me alone and grieving.

I went reluctantly to take tea with Opale as promised, trying to take my mind off my worries. She introduced me to her mother, who was nothing like her, and her neighbour from Norwich whom she called Freddy: a pale young man who would shortly inherit the handsome title of Viscount of Canterbury.

Secretly I admired his dark, brilliant eyes across which a touching expression would flicker from time to time. The lower part of his face, resolute and well-formed, was a great contrast to his hesitant voice in which he endeavoured to express original ideas. Just as I was getting up to go, having arranged to see her again, the young Englishman, timid and eager all at once, accompanied me to my carriage, begging me not to exclude him from our next rendez-vous in the Rue Alphonse-de-Neuville. Thinking that the problem was one of jealousy, I gently explained that we were going to talk poetry and that he could perhaps come over afterwards to take Opale home. When she came to my house she informed me during the course of the conversation that her friend Freddy had fallen head over heels in love with me and that nothing could be done to discourage him.

"Tell him that I love you."

She replied, "That wouldn't make the slightest difference. All he asks is that you agree to see him from time to time."

"And meanwhile, when will I see you again? Shall we have dinner together, just the two of us?"

"Yes," she said.

Then thinking better of it, "No, I'll come after dinner so as not to leave my mother and Freddy for too long."

She came as arranged and we spent the evening in my studio bathed in moonlight and poetry. Sometimes the four of us would go out together. Freddy was happy just to look at me, speaking in that hesitant voice which was not devoid of charm but got irritating in the end.

I wanted to spend time with Opale alone, and for a longer period, so I suggested that she come with me to Venice. As soon as her mother and Freddy left for England, we landed in the city of the Doges with a romantic enthusiasm more desired than felt— and moderated by the presence of our governess who was seated opposite us in the gondola. Wearing one of those brightly-colored elasticated bonnets, Neapolitan in origin, which, worn tipped backward, accentuated her Aztec features, she greeted this new country with glee. All that was missing from this beautiful setting was romantic adventure. She sought it in the person of a captain in the merchant marine who invited her on board and greeted her with open arms. Far from following her passionate example, by which she was unfaithful to Professor B.C., Opale and I shivered with fever—not the kind we hoped to find, but from malaria, leaving us weak for the whole duration of our stay, so weak in fact that we were unable to leave our twin beds. Opale hung a photograph of Antinous above her bedstead, making her dream of Lord Alfred Douglas. This Lord had captured her heart, but she could not marry him as she was already engaged to another whose career promised to be as brilliant as Alfred's was scandalous.[2]

However, as she did not want to lose her poet, she hatched a plot to send Lord Alfred to me in the United States hoping that a marriage of convenience between him and me would enable her to arrange everything.

After we returned from Venice, where only our governess had much joy of the trip, Opale rejoined her family in Norwich. Shortly afterwards we were aghast to learn of Violette's death. Renée "unconsolable and more dead than alive" came back to the Rue Alphonse-de-Neuville where I was waiting for her in consternation, having no idea this time what to say or do! She seemed scarcely conscious of my presence however, and shut herself up in her room where I could hear her sobbing, then chanting, sometimes all night long in a rapture of suffering which at last found an outlet in poetry.

Violette was more dear to me for our childhood memories whereas she had been Renée's friend throughout adolescence.

Worried about Renée's palour and her unwillingness to speak, I took advantage of one of her visits to Violette's sister to try to find out more about her state of mind in her absence. This would no doubt be revealed in her poems: the fever-readings lying on her table... I opened the first notebook and read:

> I alone am able to bestow nights without tomorrow.

Was she tempted by Death?... Had she contemplated suicide? I knew her method of composing a poem one line at a time: starting with a single phrase. Knowing that this fragment was awaiting completion I turned the page and discovered several verses:

> While I yet sob they tell me:

---

2. The illicit liaison between Oscar Wilde and Lord Alfred Douglas outraged the latter's father so much that he left his card at that doubly famous writer's club, covered with slanderous insults. There followed a trial which, as everyone knows, resulted in Oscar Wilde being condemned to hard labour at the height of his popularity.

In the shadow of the sepulchre where her grace
grows pale,
She enjoys the fleeting peace of that bed
Her forehead sombre, and in her eyes the dawn.

I listen, but the wind from the void blows away
brave hopes of serene infinity.
I know she is no longer in the hour I clasp,
The unique and certain hour, and I believe her dead.

Next a whole poem entitled *Epitaphe*.

Gently you passed from sleep to death
From night to the grave and from dream to silence.

And finally:

Here comes the night: I will bury my dead,
My dreams, my desires, my pain and my remorse,
All the past... I will bury my dead.
I bury your eyes among the sombre violets,
Your hands, your forehead and your silent lips,
You who sleep among the sombre violets.

Then further on:

I will cover with incense, with roses, with roses
The pale hair and the closed eyelids
Of a love whose flame burned out among the roses.

So I was included, still very much alive, in this burial: "Let the Dead bury their Dead." Saddened by this discovery, I closed the notebook.

When would she give up this role as "weeper" over a live woman and a dead one, and confide in me and all the tenderness which awaited her in vain? Perhaps she harbored a secret resentment against me since she had neglected Violette for me. Trying to hide her remorse by turning away from me, giving herself up entirely to this harrowing memory, was a just revenge. I could only wait for a sign from her. It came at last when she saw me preparing for my departure to the United States.

"I'm going with you," she declared suddenly, more perhaps through fear of finding herself alone than from a desire to be with me.

To tear her away from that room where she had suffered the most grievous pain, and on the pretext of moving nearer the center of town to facilitate our departure, we took rooms at the Hotel Regina. Leaving the Rue Alphonse-de-Neuville without regret, I remembered how several times after a scene with Renée I had watched her go, my eyes following her stooped shoulders as she walked up the street, then, touched by the sight, I would run after her and bring her back—her and her smile—a smile she seemed now to have lost completely.

Our journey was good for her:

> At last I despise you, fleeting pain!
> My head is raised, my tears are over.
> My soul is freed and your flickering shadow
> Strokes it no longer these sleepless nights.
>
> Today I smile at the wounding dawn.
> Oh wind of vast oceans unperfumed by flowers,
> With a sharp salt tang invigorate my frailty.
> Oh wind from the sea, forever blow my pain away...

Before she left France, however, she had given our governess the go ahead to get ready a little apartment which Violette's sister had told her about. Renée had rented this apartment at 23 Avenue du Bois, where she had spent so much time already. This is how she described it to *The Friend:*

> Let us flee, Serenity of my ravaged hours
> To the depths of twilight, weary and barren.
> In the evening, grown tender, softly will I tell you
> Of the beauty of the only Mistress in this house.
> Oh the sharp scent, the bitter music
> Of joy extinguished never to return.

She got off the boat with me in New York as vacant as a sleepwalker who no longer feels the weight of his own body. Arriving at Bar Harbour, we were greeted by a friend from the summers of my early youth. Barely adolescent, we would wander all day long by the sea, in the mountains or the woods. When we left Eva's house, turning our backs on our family homes, her brother, a sensitive artist, would watch how our long hair, red and blonde, rippled about us, stretched out in the sun or flowing in the sea breeze.

One day, when I was waiting for Eva to finish combing her prodigious hair, which swept down to her ankles, and marvelling at its length, she suddenly seized the scissors and haphazardly hacked off a thick lock which she then held out to me. Delighted, but concerned, I scolded her for this gesture which marred her beauty. She confessed that her hair was her rival, for people were always admiring it and ignoring her; getting rid of even a small hank was not sacrifice but revenge!

This strange young woman with the sea-green eyes looked like a medieval virgin with her hair pinned up above her pale face and delicate neck, bowed down by their weight. Their blood red color seemed to feed off her, to the point of making her anaemic. She had, however, just passed her exams at Bryn Mawr with flying colors.

Eva was as retiring as Renée; they managed to spend their evenings together so that they could continue to study Greek while I went to all the society functions, as my parents wished, in order to silence certain rumors which were being spread about me from Washington right up to the Bar Harbour peninsula. (Curious coincidence, the boat which brought us here was called the 'Sappho'!)

After the dinners and balls, where I managed to enjoy myself as I have the art of repartee down to my finger tips, I would join my two friends at Eva's with a light dancer's step. Often I would arrive so late that day would already be breaking in the tower to which they had retreated. Since it seemed like a waste of time to go home and sleep, we would go and bathe instead in Duck Brook, where a babbling spring formed a series of little ponds whose clear water was not so cold as the water in the sea. In that sheltered place we would stretch out on the banks, warmed by the sun, knowing that no one would disturb us so early in the morning. Realizing that we were rather a pretty sight, we brought a Kodak along to take pictures. But as we took turns, one of us was necessarily excluded... An omen? Our nymphlike frolics were interrupted in the middle of the season by a telegram informing Renée that some close relatives, an American woman with whom we had stayed in London and her 'debutante' daughter, would be arriving at the smartest hotel in Bar Harbour where a room had already been reserved for Renée, who would thus find it easier to guide them around the social whirl. Since the social whirl was then in full flow I often had barely time to exchange despairing glances with Renée over the shoulders of our partners. Poor Renée, she hated putting on an evening dress and guiding the debutante, for whom, with my help, she had to find partners, through the quadrille!

When our duty was finally done we arranged to meet each other, Renée, Eva and myself, at Bryn Mawr where Eva had kept on her rooms. When we arrived, fall had already fired the beautiful Pennsylvania countryside with the brilliant colors of its decline. Renée wandered in the woods, seized once again by the idea of death, and with death in her soul at the thought that we would soon have to part: she to accompany relatives to England, I to join my family in Washington. This return to our various folds would have seemed unbearable had we not been fortified by the hope of seeing one another again in Paris. In the meantime Renée sadly continued her lonely walks around the College after the literature classes given by the finest and most erudite professor there, Miss G., to whom I had dared show my English poems. She encouraged me, even going so far as to invite me to her apartment where, sitting on a stool at her feet, I would read poems I had composed for her. After these stirring sessions I would go and join Renée. One evening it took me a long time to find her for she had discovered an old graveyard and the haunting death of Violette had kept her there. Despite my efforts, and her attraction for Greece, she fell once again victim to that melancholy in which only death seemed an attractive prospect and a source of comfort.

We parted shortly afterwards in tears. She, after doing her social duty in England, to move into the new apartment which awaited her in the Avenue du Bois next door to Violette's sister, I to spend the long winter in Washington with my parents as promised. I took up my old social round of visits, balls, flirtation, horse rides around the capital and confidences to my old Embassy friends, until the sudden arrival of Alfred Douglas whom, in a moment of enthusiasm, I had once described as follows:

> The whimsical profile of a page,
> Hair of gold, a dreamy brow
> and blue eyes, blue as a flower
> opening its heaven in this face.

Although he enjoyed the protection of a cousin at the English Embassy, my parents would not allow me to receive him. I was therefore reduced to driving him in my carriage through the surrounding woods. I had to advise him to leave this hostile country and return to Opale, who loved him still, whereas I had no desire to get married on any condition despite Opale's insistence. She reproached me for not considering her 'Prince Charming', her 'golden boy good enough for me'.

As he listened, Lord Alfred nervously twisted a little ring which Opale had placed upon his finger. He soon returned to her and she, on a sudden impulse, ran away with him.

Unable to attend their wedding, or the birth of their son—whose godparents Freddy and I were to be—we wondered what present to give the child. We decided upon a set of opals which he could use as marbles.

This unfortunate child, handsome but half-mad, had no need of those unlucky stones to go the way of another Douglas, for he killed himself upon reaching puberty. Opale and 'Bosie' continued to live together, more for worse than for better.

A little while after Alfred Douglas' unfortunate stay, I was visited by a young Frenchman, the Comte de la Palisse, a rather shabby-looking fellow. He said he had been sent by our governess-chaperone, who had introduced me to him in Paris and "had led him to hope that I would accept his attentions." Realizing what he had in mind I immediately discouraged him. His behavior astonished me nonetheless, induced as it was by a schemer who, hoping to oust Freddy whom she considered my English suitor, had urged her unfortunate protege to try his luck and undertake that expensive journey, with its prompt return trip.

I wrote to Renée but with no reply. According to Mary S., she had moved not into the little apartment which had been prepared for her at such expense by our governess, but into the large one on the ground floor. Mary S. only saw her in passing as Renée was totally absorbed in decorating it in a highly original style. Was it her interior decorating which prevented Renée replying to my letters? Or was it the launch of her new book, *Evocations*, of which she had sent me a copy? I was worried and looked to this book to explain what could have provoked her silence. I found some reassurance in her poems "for Atthis"—Atthis being one of her nicknames for me—but was surprised to be referred to in the past:

> For I remember the divine anticipation,
> The shadow and the fevered evenings of the past…
> Amid the sighs and the burning tears,
> I loved you Atthis.

There followed several verses of description, then this last verse:

> Now my sob is heard and rises with the flame,
> And the soaring of songs and the breath of lilies,
> The deep-rooted sob of the soul of my soul:
> I loved you Atthis.

What prevented such strong feelings from enduring? I was in a fever of impatience and apprehension, bound as I was by my duty toward social frivolity and without resources of my own with which to escape. I returned at last to Paris in the spring with my family. Before setting foot in my bedroom at the Hotel d'Albe, I rushed over to the Avenue du Bois where the concierge informed me: "Mademoiselle went out a while ago."

I waited in the large courtyard at number 23. My heart beat wildly as I caught sight of her at last in her car. I was running to meet her when she ordered her chauffeur to drive on out the back way without stopping. Was it possible that she had not seen me? I

ran up to Violette's sister's apartment. Mary greeted me kindly
but either could not or would not explain the mystery. I stayed
there for hours hoping that Renée would come up unexpectedly. I
stood watch from that apartment just above Renée's in case she
should appear in the little garden. Fearing the treacherous governess might have intercepted the letter in which I announced my
arrival, I wanted to get to the bottom of the matter and, indeed, I
had my answer that very evening. Renée appeared in the garden in
the company of a very large individual; the manner in which this
individual placed her arms around Renée's person made the intimacy between them quite clear. She had evidently made a conquest of Renée, but how? Certainly not by her physical charms.
Perhaps beneath all that flubber lurked not only the overbearing
face of a Walkyrie but also a heart of gold? Renée had never
aspired to all the useless luxury with which the new arrival surrounded her, her personal fortune having always more than suf-
ficed for her needs. Who was to profit from this prodigality if not
our artful governess?

If only I had been certain that Renée was happy, I would have
slipped away unnoticed; but why had she bothered to send me her
new book, which she knew I would read and in which I could feel
that her love for me had not died? Rekindle it? Did her flight from
me betray weakness or only a constraint imposed from outside?
Should I write poems in reply to hers, in the same spirit and with
the same Sapphic rhythm?

> I wait for her, I keep vigil...
> I hope in vain, I count the seconds,
> And know not what to do. Oh double thoughts!
> For what new love are her unfaithful glances,
>
> Her braided locks?
>
> Oh night who unites parted lovers
> You most merciful, most often beseeched,
> Can you lead back to my heart the cruel
>
> Heart of my beloved?

Hating to suffer as much as I hated causing suffering, I observed that instead of laying me low it forced me to show what I was made of. Riding my horse past Renée's window one day, I noticed that when another mount tried to pass me, with one accord my horse and I leapt off at a wild gallop to avoid being overtaken. These reactions are, perhaps, a question of breeding.

But how could I win her back? Should I bang on her closed door? Dare to send her a more direct poem, reveal to her my suffering, how much I was suffering? Swallow my pride and admit that I loved her still, since I could not help but be faithful to her?

> No longer trying to please or even move you,
> Let me draw near you, more virginal
> Than the snow: teach me your impartial peace,
> Destroy my will and my power.
>
> I want to hide my eyes, sadder than the evening,
> From your eyes, forget everything save the small oval
> Of your face and, with my forehead on your soft breasts,
> Sob out my hopeless tears.
>
> My tears are a slow poison I will drink
> Instead of gleaning from some trivial affair
> A barren cure, the final numbness.
>
> Near you, my desire burns up in disillusion.
> Oh regret! How keenly I still feel the pain
> Of dreaming of a joy in which I no longer believe.

But how to get this sonnet to her without anyone else reading it? I asked my friend, Emma Calvé—who was also suffering from a romantic desertion and whom I had tried to comfort during her triumphant tour of the United States in *Carmen*, to lend me her irresistible voice. That night, disguised as street singers, she sang under Renée Vivien's French windows: "I have lost Eurydice, there is no pain like mine," while I pretended to pick up coins thrown to us from the other floors. At last Renée opened her French window, the better to hear that astounding voice singing the famous aria. "Love is a Bohemian whom no law binds." The moment had arrived. I threw my poem, attached to a bouquet of flowers, over the garden fence so that she would see it and pick it up. But passers-by were beginning to crowd around us and we had to slip away before the singer, recognized even in the shadows by her voice, was swamped with applause.

I soon got a reply to my sonnet. Not from Renée as I had hoped, but from the governess who, having gathered up both poem and bouquet, "destined for a person whose welfare was her concern, begged me to cease these dispatches which were as useless as they were distressing."

If it is true that feelings cannot be summoned to order, it is truer still that they cannot be dismissed to order! My rage was only equalled by my anguish. I sent an SOS to Eva who came immediately. Horrified to find me in such despair, she went to plead my cause with Renée, who saw her several times and even made advances to her but obstinately refused to speak to me. By all appearances this existence suited her ("Since it is, apparently, necessary to live") for she knew I was obsessed by her flight from me and haunted by her poetry while she, inspired by my memory, need no longer be agitated by my presence.

Too tormented in mind to accompany my father to Nauheim once more, I let him take his cure alone then go on to Monte Carlo for treatment in the care of a nurse, for in his precarious state of health he needed observation.

Knowing that Renée had invited Eva to join her in her box at the opera to watch Manfred, with Eva's complicity I took her place. Renée greeted me with open arms and we listened to the music of Schumann rapturously entwined, watched by the vigilant eye of the governess who was sitting in state in the corner of the box next to Levy-Dhurmer for whom Renée had just posed. As she drove me back to my hotel, Renée promised to meet me again the next day. Since the hour she had suggested had already passed, and as I had to take the train to Monte Carlo that very day, I summoned the courage to telephone her. "One cannot play one's life over again," she told me. Then, when she heard that I had just received a telegram saying that my father's health had deteriorated, she added, hesitantly, "If his health gives cause for alarm and you need me..." "I don't need anyone," I replied bravely and hung up, with death in my soul.

When I reached Monte Carlo the following morning the nurse, who was there to meet me at the station, told me that my father had had another heart attack while I was on my way to him and that he had died peacefully in the night. I had never seen death at close quarters before and I stood respectfully beside his now serene face, while the nurse told me that the night before he died he had had a happy dream in which he saw a room full of flowers for my wedding. So, right up to his last breath, my poor father had dreamed of seeing me married to Freddy.

Freddy and Eva were waiting for me in Paris. I followed my father's coffin to Père-Lachaise on my own, then my two friends accompanied me to Le Havre with his ashes. It was on a sad grey day that I boarded the transatlantic liner but, instead of bidding me farewell, they decided with one accord to make the crossing with me. My mother, my sister and one of my father's brothers were there to meet me in New York. Once the funeral ceremonies and estate formalities were over, I left for France with my two companions. There Eva and I moved temporarily into Freddy's apartment at 4 Rue Chalgrin, almost opposite Renée's house.

There was very little furniture in this apartment—two divans, a sofa and a few chairs, all of which had still to be covered, and, rare treasure, a large Boule table.

Freddy preferred to stay in a hotel, not wanting to live in his apartment until it was fully-furnished—but would it ever be? He demanded such perfection: handmade sheets of Irish linen as fine as his handkerchiefs; curtains of I forget what silk; carpets from the lost Orient; a collection of "fleur de capucine" porcelain; China cups "à la lune ravie," silver gilt spoons, each with a different decoration made by the same jeweller-goldsmith in the Rue de la Paix where he ordered a ring—which he hoped one day to see me wear—set with diamonds and the enamel eye of a peacock at the center, to represent his coat of arms.

He noticed that I scattered my hair pins liberally about and he had some made of the same shape but of fine gold, all a standard size, so that I could lose them in city or in forest where some poor woman might pick them up, ignorant of their real value!

Absorbed by plans and schemes, he neglected to renew his wardrobe. When I pointed this out to him, he replied, "Why not be as shabby as a Duke?" Does one not need a touch of madness to live in such a precarious fashion but with such imagination?

Since I had inherited part of my father's fortune and was of the opinion that my parents had brought me into the world to live my own life rather than theirs, I took advantage of this freedom to fulfil my one ambition: getting Renée back. That's when I learned of the machinations of our governess. Taking advantage of Renée's credulous jealousy, she had persuaded her—backed by hard evidence—that one of my suitors, the Comte de la Palisse, had gone to the States expressly to marry me. How could Renée have believed such an absurdity? Since she violently repelled the slightest advance on the part of any of her suitors, perhaps she simply did not understand why I made myself agreeable, nor that I often found the company of intelligent men more interesting and more agreeable than that of a pretty woman. In some I confided quite freely, and generally behaved toward men as a friend and brother. Anyway, why these "angry looks" between Sodom and Gomorrah instead of unambiguous fellow-feeling?

A sociable, well-balanced person, I was unable to anticipate Renée's irrational change of heart and was deeply hurt by it.

Our governess' clumsy trick had nevertheless succeeded in throwing poor, unhappy Renée into the arms of another! By what chance, or by what intrigue was it that the arms were those of one of the richest women in the Israelite world? This huge, self-willed personage was known not only for her exclusive tastes but also for setting up her successive mistresses in sumptuous homes with an income for life. This prodigality did not explain why Renée who, as I have explained, had a considerable fortune, had fallen for the gilded cage. Our governess, having set up the little apartment at great expense, seeing it chosen then abandoned, next presided over the luxurious furnishing of the spacious ground floor. Everything passed through her hands and she was also generously rewarded for her role as guardian to the captive — though the captive was probably held of her own free will, having immense need of calm

and security after Violette's death and the crafty lies she had been
told about me.

I received a telegram in the Rue Chalgrin from an Austrian
Princess who was a great friend of Eva's and mine. She told me
that Renée had just arrived at Bayreuth, and that she was alone.
So we went off to the Wagnerian festival and succeeded in procur-
ing two tickets, thanks to some friends of the Princess. I sighted
Renée at the very first performance of the Tetralogy and watched
her from our balcony. Eva went down immediately to tell her I
was waiting for her up there. Renée gave Eva her seat and came
and sat next to me: captivated by the music, first our eyes then our
hands met in the shadows, and each evening found us together. As
I aspired to get her back independent of this Wagnerian commun-
ion, I had a long prose poem delivered to her entitled *Je me souviens [I remember]* which I had written for her, hoping that she
would be moved when she saw how much her loss had affected
me.

Let us forget the days of anger and the days of reason and all
that separates your hand from my loving hand.
Was it you who wrote, "I would exchange the whole of human
existence for one hour," and would you dare face the "divine
peril" of your songs?
Have you put all your courage, all your poetry into your poems
that so little is left for your life?
The evening stretches toward you, I am the evening at your
window…close your eyes… let me love you. No action is
stranger than that of the night.
Go mad with me, for madness is the wisdom of the shadows.

Since the end of her stay was drawing near, and she had not
yet responded to my appeal, doubtless alarmed by the tone of my
demands, I resolved, regretfully, resignedly, to end things:

Close by, in the middle of town, in the middle of summer,
is a sad and lonely garden which fall never forsakes.
"Will you go there with me?"
A deserted palace gazes at itself in dead waters upon which
float leaves long-withered; two swans, hostile and alike, come

and go amongst them, leaving no eddies in their wake. There is no life in this place save the reflection of things past; no other dream than memory.

"Will you go there with me?"

And that is where she met me the evening she left Bayreuth. As she said goodbye, with tears in her eyes, she promised to arrange things so that she could see me again before the end of August, the current month. We would meet in Vienna and travel on together in the Orient-Express via Constantinople to Mytilene.

This time she kept her word and my elation upon seeing her again was boundless, though I had to suppress it as she was still on the defensive. She did, however, identify me with her cult of Lesbos, writing:

> Now my soul has taken flight once more,
> Sweet mistress of my songs, let us go to Mytilene.
> ...
> Let us enjoy the welcome of delightful maidens:
> The tears of return will find our eyes:
> At last we will see the lands of lifeless love
> ...
> Grow distant.

How important the landscape was to her! While I would have been happy to be with her anywhere, away from the world, on condition that she be entirely present.

So I was less disappointed than she by our first sight of this island which Countess Sabini had described as "shaped like a lyre stretched out upon the sea." As we approached Mytilene we heard a phonograph on the port droning out: "Viens poupoule, viens poupoule, viens!" [Hey chick, here chick, c'mere]. Renée who had been waiting for this moment, standing on the prow of the ship since break of day, turned pale with horror! We remembered our pilgrimage when we trod the dust made sacred by the sandals of Sappho and her poetesses, despite modern interventions. I was careful not to point out that far from encountering the Greek profile of Sappho's beautiful companions while we were on Lesbos, we saw not a single woman worthy of her ancestry but only a few handsome dockers, fishermen and shepherds. The facial features of the rest of the population were as debased as their language which Renée found no longer sounded like classical Greek. Only the little rustic hotel where we stayed had kept its ancient simplicity, with its terracotta water pots and its good food cooked in olive oil, served by an old servant with a cloth wrapped around her head, followed by a balding, ageless dog.

The nights were more beautiful than all those which had gone before and from the first what a cry of victory I had to stifle!

> Welcome into your orchards a feminine couple.
> Island of melody where caresses abound...
> In the heavy scent of oriental jasmine,
> You have not forgotten Sappho or her mistresses...
> Island of melody where caresses abound...
> Welcome into your orchards a feminine couple.

The next day the whole island lay down before us like a bed: stretched out in the sun on great banks of soft seaweed, smelling the salt air, we continued to dream on the murmuring shores of the Aegean Sea, which Renée described as follows in her poem on Mytilene:

> When the lovers sighed weary, exhausted words,
> Throwing their bodies down on dry seaweed beds,
> You mingled your scent of rose and peach,
> With the long whispers which come after kisses...
> Sighing weary, exhausted words in our turn
> We threw our bodies down on your dry seaweed beds...

Had it not been for the phalanstery of the Levantines in their summer villas, we could have believed ourselves in the fifth century B.C. Renée acquired several medallions dating from that period, struck with Sappho's profile.

During this enchanted stay, with no mail and no memories, we rented two little villas connected by an orchard, for Renée was determined not to leave Mytilene and would wait for me there "faithfully, without moving" if I had business elsewhere later on.

"I have even less business elsewhere than you do," I imprudently replied, for this reminder made her frown, wrinkling her fine eyebrows. I continued quickly with an idea which I knew would please her. "Why don't we start our longed for poetry school right here, where young women vibrating with poetry, youth and love would come to us like the poetesses of old, travelling from all parts of the world to be with Sappho?"

Renée was indeed entranced by this prospect. She had moved into the bigger of the two villas and started work again on her translation of Sappho which was now nearly finished.

"But where is Atthis?" I asked.

"Atthis is right here," she replied, pulling *Cinq petits dialogues grecs* out of her bag, together with the manuscript of *Je me souviens* which I had given her in Bayreuth. The manuscript, intimate travelling companion of her cold cream, carried traces of the latter on its cover.

"We should have it published before it gets quite ruined."

"I wrote it for you alone."

"And as you see, it has never left my side."

Opening my little book of dialogues, I saw that she had underlined certain passages about Sappho and, intrigued, I re-read:

"Do you believe she was as irresistible as they say?"

"She was as irresistible as all who have obeyed their own nature. She is as irresistible as Destiny itself."

"Why did she only really love women?"

"Because only women are complex enough to attract her, fleeting enough to hold her. Only they can offer her all the ecstasy, all the torment…She loses us in ourselves, finds us again in others. I believe she is more faithful in her inconstance than others in their fidelity."

Leaning on my shoulder to read the book with me, Renée murmured in my ear:

"That Sappho there is you."

"What one describes in print is not who one is, but who one would like to be."

"Who we would like to be, so that 'someone in some future

time will remember us.'"

"Thanks to your translation of Sappho and the work of these poetesses, I will write a play whose plot I have already worked out. It will destroy the myth of Phaon, for Sappho will die because she has been betrayed by the best-beloved of her friends, as is fitting."

"Let us not talk of grief and betrayal in 'the house of the poet where grief does not enter.'"

One day we left our beds of seaweed to be rocked in a boat to Smyrna. Toward evening we heard the sound of an Asian flute and the bells of our first caravan:

> It is evening. We hear the caravans pass.
> The camels pace their heavy steps in rhythm.
> The bells at their necks play a muffled refrain.
> Smyrna sleeps, the satisfied sleep of a courtesan.

We knew that our mail awaited us at the hotel. Should we avoid it? But then where would we spend the night? As we walked into the hotel a parrot greeted us in a strident, mocking voice and the concierge handed us our letters as soon as we gave her our names. Throw them in the sea without even opening them? But then, worried by our silence, might not someone come here and disturb us? Would it not be better to open it and, perhaps, reply? A letter from Renée's friend informed her that she would like to come and visit this famous island with her, and asked her to meet her forthwith in Constantinople. Renée had only time enough to send a telegram to stop her taking the Orient-Express, saying that she was already on her way home.

Was it not more loyal to go and tell her she wanted to break up, than to give her the shock of learning such a thing from a telegram which would, in any case, not stop her? She was not the kind to be left or deceived without putting up a fight. She would come here, and then what scenes would we have to put up with? I suggested that we hide ourselves "anywhere away from the world."

"She would alert the consulates, the secret police of the whole world. Her power, like her fortune, is limitless. And even if you went away and I let her come here, instead of tiring of this kind of life she would cling on and, if she suspected something, she would move into your place. And that I could not bear."

So we had to leave in order to come back and live here in peace to develop our illustrious plan without fear or constraint. Meanwhile we had to resign ourselves to getting back on the boat which brought us here. The faithful servant, followed by her big bald dog, served our last luncheon in the orchard. We picked figs from above our heads, warmed in the sun which shone so cruelly on our departure. Renée, wanting to eat only the figs, gave her meal to the dog which, up till then, she had endeavored to avoid. Astonished by this gesture I reminded her that she loathed the beast.

"Yes," she replied, "I hate the dog as much as ever, but why should it know that?"

What compromises would she not countenance in telling her friend, who was so dear, that she wanted to leave her?

I hardly noticed the places we passed through on the return journey, for I was travelling not so much to discover a country as a person: I saw and felt everything through her eyes. My vision was troubled most acutely by a cloud of doubt which hung over me and grew to the point of anguish at the parting of our ways. She went on to join her friend, I to Paris where she had asked me to find a house next to the villas I had rented in Neuilly-Saint-James. In the meantime she could live in the one which stood at the bottom of my garden, at the corner of the Rue de Boulogne and the Rue Longchamps. We need only knock down a fence to join them up, a little like the ones we had just left.

As I began to get our houses ready, I was in a state of feverish impatience waiting for Renée to come, or at least for some message, via the intermediary of Professor B.C., as arranged. He was helping her correct the proofs of her Greek translation. The first one arrived at last, filling me with images of a disillusioned, dispirited Renée, the victim of incurable regrets. Others followed begging me not to break her all over again, promising to "end this hypocritical, trivial life," calling me "her Inspiration," herself "glorified, transfigured, almost inaccessible, imperceptible except in rare moments of joy and grief." Then the messages stopped and Monsieur B.C. asked me to meet him so that he could put to me a delicate proposition with which he had been entrusted. He came to tell me that Renée's friend wished to go and stay on Mytilene, explaining that in this case the house rented in my name would pose "a very great risk." Renée, fearful of painful complications for herself and for her friend, whom she loved "so sadly and so tenderly," implored me to give up the house to her. She had begun to write me a long letter about this but was nearly caught in the act. Moved, I renounced everything except the memory of that enchanted island which had now lost all attraction for me. Renée's changes of heart continued for a long time. Now fleeing from me— "Siren return to the sea, because I, daughter of the Earth, have returned to the black depths..."—now assuring me of her unshakeable attachment, she kept me in a state of endless uncertainty.

Unable to live either with or without her, I do not know what I found more painful: our endangered meetings, our separations or our attempts at fidelity.

Like so many other lovers, we had not finished with those "bitter farewells which do not last" and those exhilarating but short-lived reconciliations.

Separated from each other, then irresistibly drawn towards one another, losing ourselves once again, our abiding love went through all the phases of a mortal attachment. Perhaps death was the only thing which would end it.

I loved Renée always, but with a defeated love, subject to the circumstances she had allowed to dominate us:

> Your clear-eyed glance embarrasses and disturbs me...
> Yes I know, I was wrong many, many times,
> And I blush before you, piteously,
> But everywhere I went I was hounded by grief.
> Do not blame me then! Rather comfort me
> For having lived so badly my wretched life.

Thanks to this "wretched life" and the joy which eluded her, she became what she always wanted to be: a great poet.

As I read *la Vénus des Aveugles [The Venus of the Blind]* and *Aux heures des mains jointes [Hand in Hand]*, I noticed how much stronger her poems had become. There were no more "perfumed pallors" and other insipidities trailing along. They were no longer languorous but heavy with images from her life, reflecting the cruelty of her existence against which she had at first rebelled, then borne with resignation and grandeur.

....

> My poetry has not reached the point of calm excellence,
> I realize that, and no one will ever read it...
> I am left with the moon and encroaching silence,
> and lilies, and above all, the woman I loved...

....

> On my hands remains the scent of her beautiful hair.
> May I be buried with my memories, just as
> Queens were buried with all their finery...
> I will take with me all my joy and care...
> Isis, I have prepared the funeral bark
> To be filled with flowers, spices and nard,
> The sails fluttering with the folds of a shroud...
> The ritual rowers are ready... It is growing late...

....

Renée, whose work was becoming more and more popular in many different milieux, was prevailed upon to invite a gathering of friends and admirers and we went to some very strange parties where I met up with Colette, Moreno, the Ernest Charles, the Ledrains, and our old Professor, conscientious and rejuvenated— without our governess who had long since been thanked for her various services. I was accompanied to these events by a golden-eyed actress with auburn hair and a difficult temperament. Her presence allayed any suspicion Renée's friend might have had; she never appeared at these parties but was informed of everything that went on. This is how Colette describes one of those evenings in which she danced with Moreno and recited some poetry:

> Her sumptuous, sombre ever-changing apartment has been only sketchily described. Apart from some Buddhas and antique musical instruments, all the furniture at Renée Vivien's moved in mysterious ways. A collection of gold Persian coins gave place to some jade, to lacquer work, driven out in their turn by a glass case of insects and exotic butterflies. Renée wandered

about draped in a veil rather than a gown, of black and violet, amongst these shifting wonders, in the dark of a dwelling made sombre by curtains, stained glass and heavy incense. Three candles wept their brown wax tears in a dining room, above a chinese table laden with raw fish rolled around glass rods, pâté de foie gras, shrimp, sweet and savoury salads, fruit served in jade bowls and Hispano-Moorish dishes, the whole washed down with a good champagne and exceptionally stiff cocktails. Suffocated by the dimness, my appetite cut by the three candles, I remember I once brought an unacceptable, insulting oil lamp and placed it in front of my plate. Renée cried like a little girl and then laughed...

...She gave away everything, all the time; the rare curio someone admired would be lifted off the shelf, the bracelet clasp would be opened, the scarf and necklace would be slipped off her victim neck... She seemed to be peeling off leaves. The only unexpected thing about her was her extraordinary politeness, a rather distracted courtesy and the patience, the gentleness of creatures who hope for nothing save, perhaps, for their lives to end.

I had occasion to ride rough-shod over this gentleness. Gripped by the same neurosis which is currently causing devastation upon the beauty of women, Renée Vivien wanted no flesh to weigh upon the bowed framework of her body. She lived on a piece of fruit, a spoonful of rice, and a glass of champagne, a gulp of alcohol when she was faint from starvation. Whether I was severe with her or ironic, Renée would not eat. When she inadvertently put on four kilos, she lost them again in ten days and nearly died of it.

I was lucky enough to meet Lucie Delarue-Mardrus, whom I had known before I moved into the Rue Chalgrin, which she called the Rue Chagrin, (Sorrow), at another of these *soirées*. She had returned from a distant voyage and no longer seemed angry with me for having tried to use the strong feelings she had for me, to get her to bring Renée back. She had refused point blank and gone off on her high horse, accompanied by her husband, to

North Africa and the Unknown."

We shook hands despite all our disappointments and extravagant gestures, to consolidate our friendship upon the ruins of a passion which, under different circumstances, might have succeeded in uniting us. Of what we had, which could not have been happier, I am left with a moving collection of her poems.

One day when I was at Renée's, she told me her friend, who was no longer anxious about the two of us, wanted to meet me and would be coming to dine with us. I made as if to flee, but Renée begged me to stay. Her friend would take my refusal badly. She was coming specially, wearing an evening gown she had ordered from Laferrière, which I was expected to admire, what's more. Since the meeting would make Renée's life easier, I had to resign myself to it.

While I was waiting to see my rival—who Princess H. had irreverently dubbed "la brioche"—I asked Renée why she attached such importance to matters of dress when it came to her friend, since she gave it scant attention when it came to herself?

"I prefer to leave that burden to others and decorate only my apartment..." she told me, adding, "What's more, I hate the fittings, lacking the necessary personality to carry them off. I did however try to get used to it, and ordered a dress from one of the foremost couturiers. I arrived before the hour appointed for my fitting and went and sat in a corner of the great salon until someone came to tell me it was my turn. Having brought a good book to keep me company, I read it paying no more attention to what was going on around me. But when evening forced me to raise my head toward the chandelier which had just been lit, I got up to go. My fittings assistant, beside herself, tried to stop me. Despite her excuses, only too glad to have such an excellent pretext, I replied that such oversights only happened to the best, most patient customers...I walked resolutely out the door, assuring her with a smile that I would never return..."

When the affluent personage made her entrance, her hand held out to me, I remarked how much her blue dress covered in little islands cut from a sheet of silver surrounded by diamonds, seemed to evoke the isles of the Aegean Sea; an allusion which provoked three entirely different smiles from each of us. After dinner the Chinese butler brought Renée a *tisane*, instead of drinking it she hurled saucer, cup and spoon into the fire burning before us. Despite myself, I thought of her prayer:

"Who will bring me hemlock in their own hands?"

Did she throw down the cup because it contained hemlock, or because it did not? Or because she considered the remedy pitifully inadequate for her pain?

Momentarily interrupted by the violent irritability of this gesture, we went on with our conversation about horses, in which her friend and I had found a common ground. She explained that a neighbor had asked to buy a dappled grey horse, of a race found only in her stables. It would go very well with the one the woman already owned. Should she accept the offer? She hesitated because it pained her as much to sell one of her horses as it flattered her to be asked. On this note, it being time for me to go, she offered to drive me back. Renée silently begged for me to accept.

We set off together through the *Bois* to my house. She wanted to come in with me, but I made my excuses, saying I had a terrible headache (an ill I have never suffered in my life). She left with a reproachful look.

Some time after this evening—during which she had in vain tried to teach me to smoke—the lady sent me a little enamel cigarette case full of tiny cigarettes. She had had: "Right to the bitter end, as always, Mademoiselle?" engraved inside the lid. Since I had done nothing to encourage her to send me this useless gift— unless it was my ironic admiration of her dress—I decided she was looking for an adventure. I learned soon afterwards that the neighbor who had offered to buy her horse had made a bet—in front of several people, including the woman who told me the story—"to possess not only the horse, but the owner too." I immediately informed Renée, who after making enquiries, had to admit that the neighbor in question had won her bet. Since she seemed more outraged than hurt by the affair, I tried to reason with her:

"Really, Renée, do you have the right to be so indignant?"

"It is as though I had agreed to marry a horse dealer and after sacrificing myself to someone so vile, the horse dealer were to cheat on me. I will not tolerate this insult."

Worried by her excessive reaction to this affair, which I found fairly harmless after years of exceptional fidelity on the part of her friend, I asked our professor about it—he was still devoted to Renée. He told me that she had decided to "end this hypocritical, trivial way of life." She put her plan into action: packing up her favorite curio, a jade Buddha, then closing her bank account and taking all her money out. Looking for her ticket to show the inspector on the train taking her to Marseilles, she let drop a whole bundle of bank notes in front of the other passengers. Afraid of being followed and robbed, she let herself be picked up by her friend's secretary on the platform of the shipping line. Afterwards her friend sent me a card, on which was written a single word: "Judas!"

After this defeat and humiliation, I do not know what excesses Renée had to put up with, but she did not abandon her plan to travel. She ran off again, having prepared her departure better this time, leaving with relatives for a round the world trip. I received a note from her first port of call, telling me she had sailed away, far from everything she had loved, in order to reflect on how she would continue her "miserable existence." She had been wounded on all sides and had already had her books withdrawn from circulation because of some malicious reviews.

This back-biting and other attacks magnified by her imagination, were the inspiration for three of her finest poems: *Sur la place publique [In the Town Square]*, *Le pilori [The Pillory]* and *Vaincue [Beaten]*.

Given the results, I could not criticize her for being over-sensitive and over-susceptible. By precipitating her separation from her friend, I might have administered the fatal last drop of bitterness. I feared for her health, which was already so weakened and could not withstand the slightest shock or reproach. As for me, I had been facing disgrace for years: I considered it the best way of getting rid of nuisances. Nothing frees one from the whole breed like a good scandal. Withdrawn from high society—before it could withdraw from me—I ended up seeing only people of my choosing, and of an inexhaustible variety: ranging from a great courtesan, to a virgin poetess, from an eccentric Englishman to an exacting actress, from an elderly diplomat to an incorruptible writer, and from a great lady to painters, sculptors and musicians, whom I served as best I could. Without counting the joyous welcome given to friends old and new in Paris and in Washington. Among them, I was fondest of J.L. for, instead of following his father into politics, he chose the arts. His great devotion remains dear to me, as well as the poems he wrote me, entitled: *Alcée a Sapho. [Alcaeus to Sappho].* Each time I went to America I would take refuge in his office at the Art Gallery of which he had become director, and talk to him for hours. I have most pleasant memories of those times. "Happy to forget the ones who are excluded," I took their censure lightly, more lightly than Lucie Delarue-Mardrus who wrote:

> In you, so small and frail, I see the ransom
> Of the cowardly turn-coat world
> Which judges and hides
> All instincts and thrill.
>
> Your vice, your egotism, I esteem!
> Generous and crazy you are
> What you are
> Without posing, sham or shame.

I had hoped to get Renée to adopt this attitude and, under our influence, she wrote her *Dédain de Sapho [Sappho's Disdain].*

> You who judge are nothing to me,
> I have looked too long upon the infinite shadows,
> I take no pride in your flowers, have no fear
> Of your calumny.
>
> Nothing can soil the dazzling foreheads
> Which touch my breath and my broken songs.
> Like a statue in a bustling crowd
> My soul is serene.

It was during this calm phase that she wrote me her mea culpa:

I did not understand you very well, and I was not good at loving you. I could not conquer my jealous soul. I could not overcome the resentment, mistrust and hatred which magnified and corrupted my wretched passion. I was the bitterest, most basely suspicious creature which ever made itself odious to its own self. I harassed you as I tortured myself with a thousand refined torments. I was the hangman of my soul. For everything which was unworthy of you, unworthy of me, I beg your forgiveness kneeling infinitely before you.

Then her torments started again. Having broken off all contact with her publishers, she sent her new poems to our professor and to me. I received the following confession:

I have ruined my heart, devastated my soul,
And today I go begging for love.
By the harsh light of day, the memories gnaw at me
Like the mouths of unspeakable vermin.

I have ruined my heart, devastated my soul,
And like a coward I come, imploring destiny
For the glint of caprice exquisite in your eyes.
I have searched for your look in strangers' eyes,
I have searched for your kiss on fleeting lips:
The vine which reddens in the orchard sun
Poured out the Bacchantes' laughter as it flowed...

Uncertain sweetness plucked from the fates,
So prodigally, so abundantly loved,
I have lost your smile's exquisite caprice;
Today you have made me go begging for love
Laid out in the harsh light of day
The beautiless suffering of unspeakable pain...
I have ruined my heart, devastated my soul.

I could neither recognize nor console her in this distress. Moving from despair to despair, interspersed with rare intervals of happiness, her life was nothing but a long suicide from which I tried in vain to save her, but was she not predestined for it, since everything turned to dust and ashes in her hands?

If she could not succeed in her own life, she did, according to the laws of compensation, succeed in assuring her survival.

Our professor, for his part, showed me poems which were as direct as a cry of pain:

> A victim of existence, this vicious pain,
> I address my sad appeal to infinity.
> ....
> Weary of these endless days which get no better
> Let me go away at last, anywhere, but elsewhere.
> ....
> No longer to torture myself, no more become enflamed
> To love no longer, ye gods, no more to love.
> ....
> Oh but the road is long and the evening far away.
> Since my memories grow unfaithful
> Let me flee at last on borrowed wings.[3]

Then she addressed me,

> For her whose name caresses and astounds me
> She who was love for me, when I was young.

These last verses:

> The universe seems to me like a bad dream...
> Who will tell me upon what dark road I walk?

> Who will tell me why my heavy heart is breaking
> From cold horror of Things Misunderstood?

> The rainbow of Hope has dropped from my eyes.
> Who will tell me why I tremble towards evening?

> As I listen to the wretched earth groaning
> I feel, toward evening, the full horror of being born.

---

3. After her death, these poems appeared under the name *Haillons [Rags]* for she had made it up with her editor and sent her poems to him with this letter: "I am sending you these poems with the same naive confidence with which the Japanese poets entrusted their poems to the mercy of the current, carefully placed upon the leaf of a water lily." Her poems found a safe harbor and were all collected by Alphonse Lemerre in two volumes entitled, *Poésies complètes de Renée Vivien [The Complete Works of Renée Vivien]*

I know… A hard law, perhaps. But it is the law.
But you, in all this dreadful dream? And I?

Visiting her once, probably just before she left for the Orient, Marcelle Tinayre described her thus:

> She came in like a ghost. Already very ill, she wanted to see me again…Her body, even frailer than of old, reveals nothing of her figure under her very simple black muslin dress. Alas how much she has changed! The young woman of 1899, whom I still recognized instantly! And what grace! What distinction! What simplicity there is about her, none of the odious aesthete or the literary monster! She has created a decor, not for others, through artistic vanity, but for herself as the embodiment of her dream.

> I will always see her, a shadow among shadows, speaking not of her life, but of her soul. She talked of the other world… And suddenly she said, "When I am so sad, so lonely, so ill, I think I would like to die a Catholic. It is the only religion in which there is beauty and poetry…" And she added, with a smile…"But no priest would let me keep my little buddhas…"

What a contrast with the artificial Renée Colette describes in *Ces Plaisirs!*

Though I felt her despair was beyond human succor, I wanted to leave my house in Neuilly and wait for her to come back in a different place where no bad memories would assail her. I began to look for, and finally found, a house with a courtyard and garden, in Rue Jacob. There I became the vestal of a little Temple of Friendship. In order to escape the moving process, I went and joined the actress I had been so relieved to see the back of. As soon as I arrived in Saint-Petersburg I learned that I had been ousted: first by an attaché at the French Embassy, then by a Russian colonel. When I was about to board the train for the long return trip, an old diplomat friend of mine, who had informed me of my misfortune, brought me a copy of Voltaire's *Candide*.

Scarcely was I settled into my new home but I heard that Renée was sick. "Her illness punctuated by a series of anguished fits, and that she did not wish to see anyone." I went to see her anyway that very evening to find out how she was, a bouquet of flowers in my arms. Opening the door a crack, a butler I had never seen before informed me, "mademoiselle has just died." I had only the presence of mind to insist that they lay my violets next to her. Then I staggered away, back to the Avenue du Bois and fainted on the nearest bench.

When I regained consciousness I went home and shut myself up in my bedroom. Unable and unwilling to see her dead, I needed to get into contact immediately with all that I had left of her. Like a grave robber I fell upon the precious casket she had given me. The key was lost and I had to force the lock. It held so many tangible memories that I felt her presence around me. No one could stop her from joining me now. May I be forever haunted! For if the haunting stopped, what would be left? Oblivion. But what lover, what poet would want that?

I immersed myself in all those relics: the manuscript of poems she had written for me came back to life—a wavering life— through my tears.

A cold wind from just before dawn and the rain on the windows interrupted my reverie and awoke me to reality. Flee the confusion of all these ruined treasures? How and why was I to regain my equilibrium? Should I turn away from this past which could not live on without me? from the wandering soul of the dead woman? or welcome her in, live for her as before, and draw inspiration from her, better than before? Did I have the choice? I wrote down what I saw and felt that haunted night, as though I were a medium:

> I fear the sobbing wind and the silence obscure.
> Life is uncertain and death is not secure:
> A ghost stands before me in the shadow of my wall.
> —Oh the Past! throwing shadows on my wall!

> Awakened by this specter wandering from its tomb,
> My heart, which I had thought impregnable and hard,
> My heart has reopened under the wound of old.

> And I say your name again in the pure and fiery breath,

And I hear the wind blow in like a murmur
Of your voice: Can the Past become what is to come?
—What was the Past, can it be what is to come?

Two days later I attended her funeral as though walking in my
sleep, for I would not find what I was looking for at her graveside,
but elsewhere and within myself.

I reread the poem she had written for her tombstone:

> Here is the gate through which I leave...
> Oh my roses and my thorns!
> What matter now days gone by?
> I sleep and dream of things divine...
>
> Herein lies my ravished soul,
> It is peaceful, sleeping now
> Having for the love of Death
> Forgiven the bitter crime of Life.

I translated them into English the better to immerse myself in
them.

There were two versions given of her last words: one Catholic,
the other secular. In the past she had written:

> If the Lord were to bend over me in death,
> I would say: Oh Christ, I do not know you.

On her deathbed she is said to have murmured, painfully swal-
lowing the host: "This is the best moment of my life."

Louise Faure-Favier wrote in the *Mercure de France,* on the
other hand: "She died quite simply, murmuring the name 'Lorely'
whom she had loved so much. She was also heard to say: "I do not
regret having written beautiful poetry."

Perhaps these two contradictory accounts, which refer to different periods of her life, were each equally true. Perhaps at the
end of her life her extreme debility prevented her from saying anything at all.

The Woman who Lives with Me

I.

She came to me because her life was broken, and nothing mattered much.

They told me she was unhappy, she told me nothing, she only laughed.

I understood her because she is beautiful, and because I always understand beautiful things.

I spoke to her of her beauty and of my understanding, she listened, and sometimes answered.

Perhaps I told her that I loved her. I do not remember, I say these words lightly, for me there is no meaning left in them.

I think she knew this, and I felt a little annoyed, and very much more at my ease.

I was glad she did not care about me, it let me care very much more; if she had noticed this I should not have been pleased—it would have made my feelings responsible. I hate responsibility; she likes it. She has two children. They are not very much like her; they are little boys, and she is almost a woman. I suppose she is almost a mother too, but I never think of her as a mother; perhaps I should, women are generally nice mothers to even those who are not their children. I like her children inasmuch as they are like her, or whenever they behave like little girls. This happens often, for they have sensitive, fantastic natures, and are afraid of almost everything. *They* do not know why, *she* does—that is the great difference between them!

II.

If she has suffered much she has never told any one, it has stayed

in her silences, in her voice, in her laugh, and in the beauty of her
face.

I hate a beauty that is written in the major key. It is insolent, joyous, it shouts at you; her beauty is always there, but it is like a
sphinx, it waits to be spoken to. I do not wish to guess its secret. It
is enough that it should have one.

III.

I am not curious, neither is she; we never speak about the past,
nor wish to read each others letters—those that each of us send to
others. Our present is self sufficient, it is complete in itself. In certain moods I pretend to be jealous, and this is foolish, for she loves
nothing, and she knows that I know this.

If some day she should love something, I should lose her, and yet
should I be jealous?

IV.

For some time she has been my mistress, because she does not care
enough to resist, but she has never *given* herself to me. Perhaps she
will never give herself to anybody. Perhaps she is too limitless to
be possessed. I fear that this is so, and sometimes I hope it.

I lie near her for many hours in the day and in the night, but I
never dare to kiss her lips, and she never holds me against her
heart. Yet I suppose I am her lover, and she is *living with me.* She
has said this to convince me or to convince herself of its truth:
some truths are hard to realize. I wish she would learn to lie to me,
it would make things less real: easier.

If she lied to me I should forget her. I have almost forgotten all
the rest...I have loved many women, at least I suppose I have.
They occasionally write and tell me so, and that they miss my
love. I do not miss theirs, I only love the love I *give.* I appreciate
it—it is *mine*; the love that others give is never our own, or only
for a little while. Yet at times I have wanted it and not found it,
and most of all when it was present.

I love the love of those who are far enough away, it becomes whatever I wish to believe it.

I love the love of the woman I live with: it is always *far enough away.*

V.

We have no scenes: we do not care about the same things.

Once in a while she plays to me (she listens to the music—I to the expression of her eyes). We both like this—we have this in common, and the same things make us laugh; and this is enough. In all else one must be alone; it is best so—and yet!

VI.

She is going to leave. I asked her why. It is because she is getting fond of me, and may some day miss me when I go away from her.

I shall go away from her—I always go away from the things that I love, as well as from the things I no longer like—the former is the easier. There is joy and regret in it. In the latter there is only the regret of habit.

She likes habit for the very reason I dislike it. She may be older than I…she wishes to avoid suffering. To me suffering is still an inspiration. I prefer it infinitely to pain.

VII.

She may go back to her husband, because he is the strongest habit of her life. I do not somehow envy him this—though I wish she were my wife.

I have asked her to marry me, and in fun she has asked me to marry her. If she did, it would be merely a way of getting rid of me. She may accept it—but then someone else might become her lover. Even her husband might. I could not endure this. It is not a compliment to be asked in marriage. I have asked many women to marry me, and a great many have. It is easier to love than to like. I both love and like the woman who lives with me.

I love her passionately, for the pleasure it gives me. My love is a selfish, glorious, god-like thing. It is very theatrical. It is very magnificent. It wields words with an eloquence that few people as sincere as I are capable of. It is tearful and tender, persuasive and despotic; it has its moments of genius. She generally sleeps during these, but I am there to listen, to appreciate, and even this is enough. I am drunk, I am mad, I am happy. If she were to understand, to feel with me, we should both be; that would be the only difference. As I said before, my love—the love I give—is *self* satisfying; I wish nothing else given to me, though I should love her to love it more, so I might get drunk, mad, happy, oftener.

VIII.

She has said, "Life is as others spoil it for us." So is love. The only unforgivable thing would be for her to spoil the love I have for her. Nothing else in all the world matters to me while this lives on. I said I liked her as well, I do, but I haven't much time to think about that now, I am too absorbed in loving her, besides the other is there, it will last. Shall I care whether I like her or not when I no longer love her? It is as important to like what one loves, as it is unimportant to love what one likes.

She worries a good deal over little things, but this is not because her nature is small, but because she is sensitive. Yet I wonder why she isn't in love with me! I often wonder about this, but can find no reason why she shouldn't be, unless that in itself is one!

IX.

Last night she said to me, "I never could stand going back to him now."

I hoped I had guessed what she meant, but I asked why?

"Because…," and she held my hands very tightly and kissed them. . .and then she wept.

The End

Part Two: A Lesbian Point of View

Confidences

"I am so unhappy, my heart is in torment."

"Leis, little virgin, give me your torment or I will snatch it from your lips."

"Don't laugh, my torment is great indeed. I am sad and anxious and full of shame. On my way to meet you here I walked through the town. It was so hot that I took off my veil, contrary to the custom of my people, and the women who saw me...laughed among themselves saying, 'This must be Leika's daughter, the exiled Oriental. She still has no young man.' Then they whispered so I could hear them better, 'She's still a virgin, though she's old enough to know about love.' And they all looked at me with derision. And the men...looked at me too, but in a different way, with strangely tender, cruel little eyes, and they showed their teeth as they whistled, 'She's exquisite!' And I blushed, feeling hotter still without...my veil, and I covered my face. Tell me, you who know so much, what can I do to stop blushing and how can I lose my virginity?"

"Stay a virgin, Leis. That's worth more than anything in the world."

"I beg you, tell me. I don't want to be laughed at when I walk through the town."

"Don't walk through the town then."

"Why did they laugh if, as you say, it's better to be like me?"

"Pity them. That was envy talking."

"They said I didn't even have a husband."

"That's because they have had more than enough of husbands, little virgin!
"Oh little one, how can I make you see that nothing equals the pride of belonging to oneself, to oneself alone? Not to know the degradation of belonging to another; having been the mistress of slaves and the slave of the masters! Every man to whom you give yourself, or...who takes you, takes away a part of you until all you have left is habit and the imprint of the desire of the other. Believe me, life is an expense of self as loathsome as it is fruitless! Leis, little virgin, how I love the unspoilt freshness of your gaze! and your pure body which has never known the body of another. Oh, to feel that one has served only to slake desire, that one's beauty was given as a grazing right to those who cannot even appreciate it, since their first impulse is to defile it! It's not even that which excites them, but the realization that I am an object of value since I bear its brand: that emblem of vanished beauty. Men desire me most because others have desired me before, and they will desire me even more when there is no longer anything desirable left...I feel so good, lying next to you, Leis! I feel as clear as crystal when I touch you..."

But either Leis was not listening, or what she heard was something completely different, for after a while she said,
"Oh! Dorica! If I had your jewels, your men, your glory I would die of joy!"

Brute!

She

You love me! You love me!... If I do not yield to your desire, it is because I love you...entirely because I love you. Please understand, I want so much for you to understand me! So many men have possessed me without understanding me, that I want someone to understand me without possessing me! All the days of my life I have dreamed only of Love, I have lived for Love, for Love pure and simple, and that is the one thing I've never found. I've always embraced one of the forms of love but never love itself. I have looked for it everywhere but believe the aging smile upon my lips which know no more of its kiss than if they had never touched other lips! Do not imagine that I set any limits on my quest. I have searched barefoot in the streets and decked in golden tunics in the houses of kings. I have sought it in crime and in art, and in the one I found only a little courage and in the other so much vanity...

You want inexpressible joy, you will have it, more exquisite than you can imagine. You will unwind not only the veils from my body but also the veils from my soul; you will watch not only the rhythmic swaying of my hips but all the subtle shifts of my mind. You will possess me in every way except that in which others have possessed me... No, don't come near... No, not that...I want to stay fresh for you and forever virgin like an untapped spring...Do you want that?

He

I want your body.

Courtesan

"Do you think you can possess me for two silver plates? You are handsome, son of Ermotes, but your beauty is insufficient for a courtesan. Your mouth is full of kisses and your hair is full of perfume, but kisses and perfume blow away... My youth was cloyed with such things... You offer me your heart; what is your heart, that thing which beats for the pleasure you expect from me?... Your tears then? Morose expression of your frustrated desire. No, no, all this is nothing to me...keep it...and fill my house with your father's wealth instead... Cold stones will inflame me more passionately than your eyes...and a floor paved with rubies would delight my feet more than all your blood shed upon it... Remember, son of Ermotes, how much firmer my breasts seem to you through cloth of velvet, how jealous you were as it caressed my flesh like a lover... Keep back, son of Ermotes, only virgins get raped! My weak body, undulating knowingly, slips away from your persistent strength clumsily hardened by desire... Do not squeeze my lips between yours like that, I cannot taste the pleasure of your tongue and I will not look so beautiful when you've licked off my rouge!... Oh no, tears silver your temples...your whole body sobs and you want me to love you! Rather than battering at my closed knees, go and fill your two silver plates with gold...and, in exchange, I will bestow upon you one fake spasm...perhaps!"

The Unknown Woman

And then the unknown woman—persuasive and fearsome, sweet and terrible, turned to me and said, "If you love me you will forget your family and your husband and your country and your children and you will come and live with me. If you love me, you will leave everything you cherish, both the places you remember and the places you long to go; and your memories and your hopes will be nothing but desire for me. If you love me, you will look neither forward nor backward, you will know me only, and your destiny will carry my footprint alone. If you love me, infinity will be my lips, you will have no prison but my arms and all your desires will be for my body."

And, sobbing, I replied, "I love you."

Breasts

(A considered response to Ramon Gomez de la Serna and what he says—and does not say—about breasts.)

Dedicated to man, who is never fully weaned.

Young Spaniard, in search of hemispheres new—like your ancestor before you—what have you discovered of the mystery of these New Worlds? You have situated them on the great female body, described some of their properties, offered a few personal, at times contradictory observations on their sensitivities, flavor and climate, but they remain as strangers to you.

Why did you not ponder the attraction of breasts more deeply, young man who writes too much and too little? What are those "poultices," those insensitive "gourds" which fill your mind and trouble you so pointlessly? Those breasts out of keeping with the rest of the body? Those rapturous deceptions? Do we conclude from your exposé that only women of the north have amorous, vibrant, demanding, electric breasts, leaving southern women the animality of teats devoid of compensation? You, who have devoted yourself to breasts, and have obviously misconstrued their locality—extinguished globes, whose switch seems to have been removed! What are those dead batteries, those electric wires with no current, those bells which no longer sound?

Do you not arouse them by your touch even to the dangers of joy?

Let us leave in peace, or to their natural functions, the dead planets full of moon's milk, and turn our attention to those breasts which are attentive to the seduction they themselves have caused!

"Her breasts rose, proud of their virginity," wrote Renée Vivien. It is to them we must pay court: they stand in judgement of their admirers, testing a lover more surely than ever Portia's caskets. (How Anglo-Saxon, that feminist trick of trying out one's suitors with treasures exterior to one's person.)

Many women give themselves more willingly than they give their breasts—to avoid offering their breasts?

Those peaks, difficult of ascent, reserved for the elect, determine the quality and breeding of a lover so much better than any fun and games down below! For aren't the breasts more delicately connected with the center of sensation than the short-circuit of sexual climax? Breasts: passion's accelerator, electric lead, guide to femininity wherein the first signs of arousal dwell.

"Breasts erect as though full of milk eternally, pointing toward the sky."

Flower of the senses, complex, dense, heavy with all your secrets, language, experience, throbbing, perfumes, sight, touch; all sharpen to a point till this pre-eminence abdicates in favour of that excess which will extinguish it.

That head thrown back, those eyes which change colour and moisture, that mouth which reveals its secret source, that ardent malaise, that enticement to possession…Those breasts which sound the alarm, those cries of joy so like the cries of a newborn baby!

Bend over, attentive to this joy before *the* joy where promise and desire go hand in hand and meet to plot their own defeat!

This moment alone is yours.

Now inhale with all your being that which distinguishes love and makes it divine.

Blasphemous man who has compelled me to spell things out in this unworthy speech, may this rivalry honor and enlighten you.

Defending the breast against your masculine errors and incomprehension, I feel as though I am in some way defending my native land!

The Climbing Rose

As she looks at the dates she realizes with surprise and dismay that, despite our careful calculations, her husband might already have returned from his long journey and she turns on me with hostility. I was wounded by her injustice, and to make plain to her the wrong she did us—or perhaps simply to put her to sleep—I told her a story resembling our own in which I compared her to a climbing rose with its roots in one garden but who blossoms in another.

He whose garden is graced by this spray of flowers, forever fresh, forever new, becomes enchanted by them. Until the day he realizes full well that the wall separates him from the life of the rose bush—that it is planted in foreign soil, belongs to an owner, and that this owner, seeing his rose bush is growing over the wall and bearing its flowers abroad, can move it away, force it to climb in his garden only, for the glory of his beds so that his friends may see, admire and compliment him. For the owner is motivated only by vanity.

But he who comes in the night to his rendezvous with the roses wants the bush for his own, even if he has to steal it. The bush is happy with him, loves him dearly. But the rose does not belong to the one who loves it best; it belongs to the one who planted it.

The Sitting Room

We left Eastbourne on roads leading south, so green in winter and so clement that the summer seems to have come back in a rush, leaving its leaves behind.

Toward evening we reach the beginning of the New Forest. An inn on the edge of the forest tempts us with its pleasing asymmetry, looking like a home from home. A blowsy landlady, merry and a bit vague (she's been drinking), shows us two rooms already occupied, apologizes to the absent guests and takes us to one with two little beds which, she tells us, is not booked till the following morning. I look questioningly at my friend, she likes the place but is not so taken with the small beds. The landlady opens the door of a room down a short flight of steps whose small size is compensated by the endless lawn which stretches away from the windows. The room seems merely to provide the frame for the big bed at its center.

"This is fine for one of us, but where will the other sleep?"

"You mean the two of you cannot manage to sleep together in a bed that's six foot wide?"

"We prefer two beds and two bedrooms."

"We must have two beds and two bedrooms," my friend insists. She finds the innocence of certain English customs unfathomable. The English see nothing ambiguous about putting two girls who are not related to sleep in the same alcove. Anxious to satisfy our absurd foreign demands, the landlady shows us a delicious sitting room full of naive knickknacks with a bow window looking onto the garden, and a folding sofa. To complete our sleeping arrangements we asked that this sitting room be included as our second bedroom. The landlady says she has no spare single bed to put in there but that one of us could sleep on the sofa, she would look out some sheets and blankets. Pleased to have saved appearances, my friend declares that she will be very comfortable sleeping there. The landlady, doubtless contemptuous of our fussiness, goes off to give instructions.

We see her again later standing at the serving table, doing the carving herself, slicing the enormous joints of cold ham, beef and mutton so that we may take our pick. She tells us, in the same vague way, that she is awfully sorry but we cannot have the use of the sitting room until ten o' clock that evening as she has promised it to a gentleman. We have already agreed to this arrangement before we realize that the gentleman in question is the same individual who had driven down with a London flapper. He refills her glass with champagne and awaits the results with sly satisfaction. As she drinks his desire becomes more evident, more brutal, more assured, the gleam in his eye predatory and male.

As we go back up to our sitting room we decide not to allow it to be invaded even for an hour by this couple intoxicated to the point of lust. And since on this island the *appearance* of virtue is always triumphant, the chambermaid, left out on the landing, goes away, silently outraged by our indignation, to tell the landlady who, perhaps fearful of our shrewdness, leads the couple away somewhere else, the enormous empty banqueting hall, maybe, which we glimpsed from the garden, or simply entrusts them to the balmy evening.

"Why not let them have a bedroom?"

That would have shocked everyone. For such a manifestly unmarried couple there remains only these sitting rooms with automatic sofas—once again to save appearances —the English version of your "sperm-stained divans." With one exception: there is no way to lock the door which is, in any case, safe from intrusion thanks to the hypocritical complicity of those who profit from the situation. "A door must be either open or closed" is a very French theory; over here either alternative is considered equally dangerous.

As predicted, we spent a very comfortable night in the big hard bed having had the—very French—hypocrisy to muss up the sheets on the sofa. One can never say for sure what are the advantages and disadvantages of a bed until one has shared it with someone else. I now had occasion to observe that hard beds set the body off to greater effect since, unlike soft beds, they do not allow it to sink down into them. Laid out on this formidable buckler of horsehair and brass, my beloved seemed to have been offered up to me as the spoils of ceaseless victories. And what war drums rolled that night, my heart sounding the alarm perforce and beating with all its might. My heavy breathing was better suited to arouse her than any alarm bell, since I desired her all the more insatiably after such tremendous, satisfying resistance.

And in the morning we drove back again.

Part Three: Natalie on Gay Life Styles

Misunderstanding

If people condemn without thinking it is because they rarely tolerate anything beyond their own personal needs.

✳

Since God made Eve from Adam's rib, everything has been abnormal.

✳

Flaubert was criticized for writing: "He wept for his lover."

✳

The Puritans who landed in America had an old law: "Ye dirty fellow that lieth with ye dirty fellow shall swing until he die."

Gide and the Others

Gide's life, a series of zigzags, is, like a flash of lightning, as illuminating as it is dangerous. His actions plot out his course in broad strokes; through the lives of others he discovers himself. He is dazzling, and disappointing, and his path is dogged by shadows. Approaching everything laterally, he finds meaning in nonsense. He embraces religion the better to distance himself from it. He makes the same use, and misuse, of marriage.

He confesses in *The Immoralist* that ever since his honeymoon he has felt an irresistible attraction toward adolescent boys. If, after long years of unconsummated marriage, he turned to adultery, it was an act of caprice, or through pure contrariness. The experiment resulted in a daughter, looking just like her father.

When his wife, driven to the edge by the accumulated disappointment and despair of her married life, burnt all the letters he sent her—as so many lies—he was inconsolable. Inconsolable, not because this gesture showed how wretched he had made her, but because he considered those letters to be the most interesting he had ever written. They must have been strange love letters indeed, empty of all desire, full of that strange love so common in Anglo-Saxon countries in which the high-thinking, little-acting lover does not deign to deflower his chosen idol with lust.

Gide's version of the medieval cult of the Madonna and the Lady, or the Lady and the Madonna, is characterized by his lack of attention to women in general and to his own wife in particular, for whom he felt an unbounded respect, so that he could indulge his innate taste for boys without hindrance. Given his "perverse" personality, he was perhaps never so fond of his wife as when he was cheating on her. Their kinship and Protestant ancestry should, however, have made him more restrained, or more discreet. Since his Puritan forebears had probably exhausted all the virtues, perhaps he felt that enough was enough?

Only the gods may do as they please. Does one not need to be very certain of one's own moral code if one wants to do without any other morality?

Nevertheless, the young Gide felt constrained, at first, to a certain amount of prudence. Thus, sitting in a cafe once with Oscar Wilde, he picked a table at the back hoping that no one would recognize him. Later, at the home of our friend, Pierre Loüys, when I suggested introducing Gide to Lord Alfred Douglas, the temptation gave him a long moment of exquisite, tortuous hesitation.

Then gradually realizing that it was his hesitation in betraying social convention which betrayed him more than his actions, he was driven ineluctably beyond himself toward whatever could serve his art and singularity. Gifted with the keenest, craftiest intelligence he realized that if he put his subtle imagination—a direct product of his temperament—to work in the service of his vices, he could increase his reputation.

When Claudel himself made the mistake of complaining to Maurice Rostand about the increasing number of homosexuals who should, according to him, be driven out, Maurice replied, "But your Excellency, in that case the salons would be empty!"

Since nature has created so many different, indeed opposite types, let us praise her for offering compensation for our common wretchedness. What is more "unnatural" than the present attempt to herd us all toward one prototype, the "robot". Let us choose for ourselves amongst those who persist in having a personality and of whom there are, like rare books, but a few examples.

Gide, while proclaiming the right to homosexuality, has done nothing to raise it above the level of heterosexuality, quite the reverse! People have told me that Gide is to be praised for playing an important role in destroying the sense of sin which has weighed on the consciences of innumerable young men with homosexual tendencies. Does this good deed offset the bad example Gide set them of promiscuity reduced to the level of erotic need? This example, which too many pederasts have followed, tends to degrade what it intended to elevate above contemporary morality and would be a good argument in favour of conformity.

There is no clearer example of how to betray what one claims to love!

If "the style is the man," how can we admire the former but not the latter? How can we not deplore the fact that such a writer could find nothing better to amuse himself in his old age than pursuing young men who spurned his advances, as in the scene in his last diary which he describes down to the smallest detail?

Protestants have, doubtless, no other confessional. In any case, it was not absolution Gide had in mind but a fresh opportunity to declare his independence. What a sordid example of freedom it gives, demonstrating the servility it imposes! If everyone is to do whatever they want, let them at least do something. Shakespeare wrote his *Sonnets,* Gide the most pedestrian of his novels. Perhaps he was unconsciously working in the name of virtue by making his vice look so ugly. Is there no one left who is good at being bad!

To return to that unpleasant scene with Victor, as he is called, it is offset to some extent by another scene where Gide, in his declining years, is sitting in the shade on a terrace in the Midi. He is happy enough with a pile of clothes on his lap that a group of young boys have entrusted to him. That octogenarian must have watched their muscled young bodies with nostalgia as they competed with each other in innocent athletic contests while he had spent too much of his life devoted to erotic interludes instead of becoming, as Socrates in his wisdom advised, "the virtuous lover" and enlightened guide of those he had loved and raised to his level.

Illicit Love Defended

Countess G. used to say, "What do I care if they love men, women or canaries!"

The great lady was surely right: only love is important, not the sex to whom it is directed. The rest is merely a question of rearing, selection and segregation of the species—our own faces a danger of quite another kind. Superstition and prejudice weigh love down. Let it be free of them—our only regret that there should be so little in the world.

Since the experiment with earthly paradise didn't work out, and earth became the "vale of tears" we know today, can God have created this world of evil with its system of man eat man, or, as in the Manichean belief, did another Power? Whether our customs derive from the gods, from insects or some other origin, nature which accepts all ways of being, absorbs them and makes them hers. The expression "against nature" has naturally fallen out of use, but we should recognize that nothing could be more unnatural than the uniformity we seek to achieve.

"Boredom was born one day from uniformity."

We have already eliminated many animal species, including the bird of paradise! But what can we do about the high birth rate which threatens the human race? The biblical injunction to "Go forth and multiply" doubtless made sense at a time when there were too few human beings to populate the earth. And now? Since neither wars of extermination nor "birth control" have been sufficient to reduce the population, why does the Host of Hosts not take it upon himself to change his slogan to "Stay home and stop multiplying"? Wouldn't that be the action of a sensible host who is careful not to invite too many people to the banquet of life (a banquet at which the food is getting more and more tasteless!) whom he's unable to receive, feed and lodge properly?

"You will earn your bread by the sweat of your brow."

But what if there are more brows than bread? And if the Creator had his reasons for wanting to destroy Sodom and Gomorrah, are those reasons still valid? And didn't he also curse the first couple by throwing them out of paradise and condemning them to reproduce in pain?

Despite its harsh beginnings on earth, the family, which forms the basis of our society, remains an irreplaceable institution, even though it often produces parents and siblings who are each other's enemies. Nevertheless, it survives for better or worse—worse in the case of many poor couples overwhelmed by misery and innumerable children.

If the exhortation to fertility persists, having outlived its usefulness, this is partly due to the prejudices which still blind many worthy people. Reforms and moral injunctions are rarely entirely disinterested. Take those virtuous militants for example who, looking for good works to occupy themselves, rarely tolerant or understanding of anything beyond their own needs, surpassed themselves by wedding social causes (no men being available). If they have failed to wipe out certain practices (despite a recent prison case reminiscent of the days of Oscar Wilde) and, if, despite having the law on their side, they encounter so many discouraging obstacles in shepherding the perverted back onto the "right road," perhaps it is because the laws they are defending are out of date.

It is often not fully appreciated that for most of the sexually abnormal, perversion would consist of adopting a normal sexual practice! People should pay more attention to those authors who have made a special study of the matter: Havelock Ellis, Kraft Ebbing, Freud, Jung, etc.... Thanks to them the hypocrisy surrounding the issue is beginning to dissipate.

But will the most advanced countries, anxious about their rising birth rates, dare to advocate what they already tacitly accept: homosexuality, that safety valve practiced throughout time, which many young people turn to instinctively even though they believe they are committing a mortal sin?

That homosexuality continues to flourish is a sign of neither privilege nor of decadence, but a simple fact which needs to be recognized. What's more, childless unions counterbalance those which are only too prolific, re-establishing an appropriate equilibrium. And the range of such unions is vast, from the limp-wristed sodomite to the closeted, self-deceiving or unaware!

As I said before in *The Trial of Sappho,* "We are nearly all composed of such a complex mixture of human qualities that in each one of us reside both masculine and feminine principles: what man is without any female attribute and what woman never demonstrates any masculine characteristics?" We are reminded of the primeval order preceding the "division of the sexes". We should not forget that Eve was made from Adam's rib, and that man, born of woman, cannot be entirely masculine. The normal man (if he exists), even if he boasts of being exclusively masculine, has been cut off from femininity and will "dream continually of the warmth of the breast". This might explain some of his tendencies, no doubt caused by the long months spent in his mother's womb.

There are, of course, some extreme cases, as far apart as the albino and the negro. No one should consider themselves safe from change, even without having one of those operations you read about in the papers, of which there are a couple of examples living amongst us. For nature bides its time before playing one of its tricks: it may masculinize the bodies of some women causing them to lose their physical charms, which they appear to have passed on to certain men who shamelessly flaunt their sumptuous breasts and bellies at the beach.

Though usually more discreet in terms of external changes, this sexual "turnabout" nonetheless has a profound impact on behavior and tastes. What about the married woman who adopted those of a gentleman of her class, fell for her lady love and lived out her days as her close companion? Should her husband, denied his conjugal rights, finding the divorce laws no protection, mourn this separation so much that he can never recover, or seize the opportunity to pay court to another such as he? ...Until the formerly united couple lie side by side again at last, two sexless skeletons in the family vault!

Amid this sexual confusion, alongside those who were unaware of their double nature, there have been others who were quite conscious of this duality, who could go either way at will: like Julius Caesar who, according to his contemporaries, was not only the wives' lover, but also their husbands' mistress.

Mlle. de Maupin, that female gallant, was quite unrepressed about expressing her true self. Queen Christina of Sweden behaved similarly, though with more mystery attached.

Male couples have a much harder time than normal couples, judging by Verlaine and Rimbaud and their *Season in Hell.* Verlaine's family, however, worried about their reputation, made a ridiculous attempt to prove that the relationship was platonic.

"You don't hide away alone together to practice chastity, but perhaps the relationship can become chaste if you love each other, because your loved one's body gains a significance which cannot be described in terms of lechery. For Verlaine, sex becomes chaste when it is dictated by love, and he never confuses love with physical need. Love is chaste, whatever its expression." [*]

Another, unexemplary, example is that of Oscar Wilde and Alfred Douglas. Each had suffered because of the other but instead of living apart after their trials, they were happy to be back together. Their rows and their life of debauchery started again immediately....

Do female couples, usually more exclusive, establish better households? Like the Ladies of Langollen who, after one had

---

[*] Rémy de Gourmont

abducted the other, "settled down" and were visited by the most intelligent members of the society they had scandalized.

And the great Sappho, did she not live in harmony with not one but several women friends? As one succeeded another they succumbed to that sweet rivalry which is more a source of inspiration than of discord, judging by the fragments that Sappho, the "tenth Muse", has left us...

Let us therefore respect these variants of the species who offer us their gifts: those singular beings who created works of genius instead of more dubious offspring, for it is known that the genius excels in production rather than reproduction. May those "blossoming peaks" of our race, whose only fruit are their works of art, console us for the multiplying mediocrity of humanity. And let us rejoice if some, outside the norm, bring a certain diversity to the species if only because they keep at bay the system of robots we are bent on creating—with that doctrine of equality without liberty, or fraternity, which would generate a society composed of people without personality.

As one biologist sensibly concludes, "It would be a waste of time for Nature to make each individual a unique human being only to have Society reduce humanity to a collection of people all alike."

In this state of general servitude, more to everyone's detriment than for the good of all since quality has been lost in favour of quantity, may love, source of individual rapture, lift us out of this civilization in which no one is civilized, or away from these civilized people who have no civilization!

For what does the so-called "modern world" have to offer us in exchange for our ever more besieged private lives? Collective emotions, stirred if not by H bombs then, in the meantime at least, by "boxing rings" where crowds are moved to transports of joy and enthusiasm, more than by any other spectacle, even a theatrical masterpiece, as they watch a pair of boxers fight until the "knockout."

May each enjoy the public, or private, pleasures they merit. But why does France, at the apex of civilized accomplishment, allow itself to be influenced by other nations who are still forming, or deforming, for who if not She can teach them how to live? Fortunately, while the Frenchman has succumbed to the alcoholic excesses typical across the Channel, and across the Atlantic, he is resisting the taboos of Puritanism as far as love is concerned—of which he is a greater connoisseur and practitioner than anyone.

But "illicit love" should not be confused with the depravity of those for whom sexual vice has become an obsession, a form of madness which degrades, tortures or ridicules a human being. A vice in which there is no trace of real feeling, love or passion.

What's more, passion has no need of the tricks practised by those whose speciality is impotence.

The moral:

If pleasure is so hard to attain, You might do better to abstain!

On the rare occasions when Colette waxed philosophical about "these pleasures," she defined vice as, "The evil we do in which we take no pleasure." Even our Anglican poet, T. S. Eliot recognized that there are "vices fathered by our heroism." Does it not take more courage to dare to be oneself than to conform to contemporary morality?…

Predestined for Free Choice

One does not always recognize oneself in one's acts, any more than one recognizes oneself in one's parents. My ancestors covered the range from Celts to Latins, Jews to Puritans—and doubtless more besides. But these contrasts, instead of creating a civil war inside me, bequeathed me an excellent sense of balance.

My great grand-parents, seeking refuge in America from France, Holland and England, participated in the formation of the United States and our War of Independence.*

Interpreting this spirit of independence in my own way, I returned to my maternal origins, and France has become my country of choice.

Paris has always seemed to me to be the only city in which one can live as one sees fit. Despite the baleful progress inflicted from the outside, she continues to respect, and even encourage, personality. In France, thought, food and love have remained a matter of individual choice where each person follows their own inclination, instead of that of their neighbors. Which is probably why the country is so difficult to govern, and so easy to live in.

I was predestined for free choice, for, contrary to the warnings given back home in the United States of "what is and is not done," I have always done as I pleased. What's more, does it not require deep concentration to catch hold of the messages of our interior being, and thus experience the mysteries of self-initiation?

One cannot, after all, judge an existence except in terms of what it has made of us, and what we have made of it. If life is to be the expression, and not the suppression, of self, have I not roundly fulfilled and succeeded in mine?

I love my life. Principally because I have been able to keep it

---

* Some of their deeds and exploits are featured in the preface to my *Adventures of the Mind.*

free, in order freely to give it. Guided by love—the kind which forces us to surpass ourselves—I have loved my fellow man, and particularly my fellow woman, with passion. That such feelings and dispositions may be seen as blameworthy or too intense, has never bothered me. That was the direction in which I developed.

That right-thinking people, making light of our precious relationships here below, have had other affinities, other predilections than mine, seems to me as strange as my singular life and attachments must appear to them. Is it natural, though, to despise love in favour of heavenly, or earthly, ambition? Love is certainly a great expense of self.

Which is doubtless why so many people find it so hard to accept or practise! Whether they scheme for honor and fame, get into cut-throat rivalry with their colleagues over career promotion (for one needs to make a living—living off others), whether they amass great fortunes or contract profitable marriages, all these attempts at "making it" have the same result: one loses oneself on the way. Consequently, almost no one lives their own true life, almost no one pays attention to the one thing which, to my mind, is essential: love. Love, the perfect median between heaven and earth—for it spiritualizes the material and materializes the spiritual in the form of our own being, blessed with both body and soul which only love can reunite.

Do not let us imagine, however, that the lover's calling is an unmixed delight: it is, rather, a continual tension in which one tries to guide and guard the one we love, exercising all one's perspicacity and charm to ensure her continued happiness. For it to last, love should be composed of all our other loves. I am, perhaps, love's mystic, though this has never deterred me from the thrill of its practice. But should we not abandon the trappings of love before they abandon us?

Being other than normal is a perilous advantage. And does one not need a more tempered courage to live one's life than to sacrifice oneself to some duty or other?

Living in the eye of love is an adventure for which few are suited. It's a very trying environment; most of those who attempt it are in danger of burning up with fever or starvation. Few constitutions survive. As for me, the striving, the pain and the mystery are more than just my native land. It is only there that I feel I am in my element…

My life is truly my own, without pretense, and so, consequently, is my work: my writing is simply the result, the accompaniment. I offer them as such.

If too little of the love I am claiming is found in this book, it is because I have spent it more profitably elsewhere. There remain only fragments here. And when I leave my natural element, I go armed as an amazon.

How can I complete this moral, or immoral, portrait?

Born to young, good-looking, healthy parents, I have never had a serious illness.

My childhood? "Extraordinary," like everyone else's but unlike everyone else, I am not set on recounting it in detail.

I am more conscious of my adolescence as a "sad, sweet little page."

If my education was nil, it is because:

"My only books were women's looks…"

My love affairs? Many.

My friendships? Loyal and faithful.

My youth? It continues, like for the elderly Goethe: how many first loves meet up with our last loves! How many chosen affinities find each other again then!

I have examined many hearts, comparing them with my own.

> "How many beauties, how much candor
> have aroused my feeble heart which, till it beat its last,
> will remain the heart of a lover."

My last heart beat, which I neither long for nor fear.

Without hatred for those who are different from me, nor for those who would be my enemy, my sensibility is such that I cannot witness suffering without suffering myself.

Naturally intuitive, I am able to interpret even the silence of children. I believe I have never approached another being without doing them some good.

My joys are quite unselfish, for I experience them only through the one I love.

To love like that is to play only for the other, stirring up wonder, demanding from life more than it gives, for it is a raw, intractable material which must be continually reworked if it is to yield more than our paradise lost.

It seems that all my journeys have been with, or toward, someone who was dear to me, and that all my letters and poems were inspired by love, or by loving friendship.

Would Renée Vivien have found her way without me?

Would Rémy de Gourmont's life have been renewed without his Amazon?

As for the portraits which follow, those who would condemn them as indiscreet, should bear in mind that all art, all artistic expression, is an indiscretion we commit against ourselves.

Discretion about the past, which is really passed, is no better than oblivion. Silence too can be indiscreet. And would it not be the height of cowardice to allow our dead to die?

If, in the course of these confessions, which are open to the heavens, I have pushed certain memories to the extremes of confidence, I hope I have never overstepped the line where indiscretion is the privilege of tact.

Part Four: A Fine Spray of Salon Wit

Scatterings

There are more evil ears than bad mouths.

*

Glory: to be known to those we would not wish to know.

*

You can tell a person's breeding by their temper.

*

I have known temptation, but no temptress.

*

You are so much more beautiful than the things that will befall you.

*

Forever is far too long.

*

To be married is to be neither alone nor together.

*

Knowing how to please, what a sign of age!

*

To have or have not, which is worse?

*

I never explain myself, I do my bidding.

*

Only I can make myself blush.

*

How frightened they must be of losing their youth who gain nothing with age.

*

To grow old is to show oneself.

One should only dare to criticize that which one admires.

*

Those who are bored by life are still richer than those who amuse themselves outside it.

*

I am most curious about myself.

*

That laughter, all on the surface, which seems not to keep any amusement for itself.

*

Sometimes we get what we want, and it is not what we wanted.

*

I do not care what you do, but who you are.

*

I only judge by their acts those I dislike. We are wearied by the work we do not do.

*

I judge people's charm by the ease with which I express myself in their presence.

*

What inner resources one must have to live a life of idleness without tiring.

*

Delicacy: that aristocracy of strength... How little they must have who call it impotence!

*

Every loss enriches me.

*

Some people make it hard for me to believe in universal evolution.

*

When joy befalls me, I am less inclined than ever to believe in chance.

Little Mistresses

Do we not only love in them what we lend them of ourselves?

⁂

To be sufficiently distracted no longer to think of everything.

⁂

Who will console me for my gaiety?

⁂

How much strength we need to yield to what we want the most.

⁂

My sorrows? I invent them, I have to for sheer joy.

⁂

"Creating literature," what a nasty reproach to life!

⁂

How horrible life is—the life of others.

⁂

I am suffering a crisis of equilibrium!

⁂

One is not oneself everyday—fortunately.

And their superstitions…

Hard times cannot last forever.

⁂

Those who go to sleep with anger will not wake up together.

⁂

As long as one is young one is ageless.

⁂

Every night I dream that you are unfaithful, but last night I finally had a good dream: you killed yourself for me.

*

She is not worth my pains to win her—my pain is worth my pains.

*

(In praise of a lover) He knew so well how not to kiss me!

*

Lace: the art of the hole.

*

Eyes to be gazed at, to receive admirers, having given up seeing for themselves.

*

Eyes sharp as barley stalks beneath arched brows—arresting eyes.

*

Proud, weary eyes—eyes which hold back tears.

*

Her current mood: to be heavy hearted!

*

Eyes so pale they seem to sap the colour from everything they look at (the eyes of a moralist).

*

Those who stare at the sun see everything bathed in gold: just so, having gazed so long into your eyes, everything I look at takes on their color.

*

To love is to see through two pairs of eyes.

*

Women pass by, freshly made up: bad paintings no one would sign their name to.

*

Fashion: the search for a new absurdity.

*

She called me "my love," the name had become a habit, spoken without feeling, the beginning of a sentence which would end quite differently; a sad domestic word from which all joy had gone...

*

Words would become little graves if we did not abandon them in time.

※

How many people have locked up their whole lives in one empty word.

※

To be coward enough to choose!

※

To have the strength and simplicity to be weak.

※

If motherhood happened backwards, starting with the pains of labour, there would still be mothers, but mothers of a different kind, willing heroines not victims of an oversight, or wretched martyrs to a trick of nature.

※

All our unshed tears are inscribed on our faces by the passage of time.

※

That refinement of suffering: to smile.

※

An express letter arrived informing one of them of the death of her hopes. A few tears rose to her eyes, then she wrapped herself up in the trappings of sorrow. She became a kind of widow without a veil, untouchable in her mourning...closed in, isolated, turned to ice almost instantaneously as people are by misfortune. To become invulnerable, untouchable, insensitive, closed in response to the blow we have suffered, is that not too much like dying with the dead?

※

Might not pain be the anvil on which one cracks only base metals?

※

Our shadows are taller than ourselves.

※

You say such sweet words to me; why are you not she?

※

How wearying it is to have enemies but no adversaries!

*

Is it really you I am talking to? I do not know, but someone I love is listening.

*

In a world of artifice walked the real gold of her hair.

*

To be big enough for happiness.

*

Which of all our pasts will be *the* Past?

*

I did not yet know it would be *you* I would love in you—I did not yet know it was *you* I would love in others!

*

I sensed he found me prettier than he feared!

*

Do you love me? I ask so that the question will occupy your mind, so that you will tell yourself the answer. For it is for your sake far more than for mine that I want you to love me.
I would like to make you the splendid gift of the love you will have for me. I cannot give myself however, to those who do not know how to take me.

*

With you I am like the nervous mother who does not know how to caress her baby, who only dares to approach when it is asleep and bends over furtively to kiss it. I love you in the shadows and solitude of myself. No doubt it would be better to show a more daily tenderness in simple little things and material detail. But one does not love as one wishes—one loves as one is!

*

The differences between us are mere details—essential details!

*

What did you see in the Salon? I saw—that I was seen.

*

She liked to look at the mirrors on her walls, the only self-portraits she had.

*

The fine veins of her temples, little blue streams under her transparent skin, seemed to have poured their colour into the irises of her eyes.

*

Weak as I am, I have strength only for passion!

*

There are women whose black eyes sparkle with energy—they make me feel so irredeemably blonde!

*

Women with an impersonal pearl necklace round their necks. A chain whose symbolism has become almost universal: the anonymous token of servility...
Those pearls are doubly distressing having lost all link with their mysterious origin by adorning the necks of so many ungainly young ladies. And yet they shimmer still, having brushed the cheeks of sirens long ago, underneath the water.

*

To be free, even if only for serial servitude.

*

How often we love what we do not like, how much oftener we dislike what we love!

*

To be beautiful, at the right time.

*

A woman: take her or leave her, but do not take her and leave her.

*

One is unfaithful to those one loves so that their charm will not become mere habit.

*

Like a city at night I have watched women pass by lit up by their jewelry.

*

How many great beauties are not beautiful!

*

It is harder to keep what you've got than to catch someone new.

*

I see her sometimes in her car accompanied by some new rose, sitting beside her on its long stalk, just like a pretty companion.

*

Why complicate our instincts with our will?

*

She was thirty-five, in other words sometimes seventeen and sometimes forty-seven.

*

To be of no particular period. Only fashion goes out of date.

*

Might I be the one I am looking for?

*

That American girl has breeding. —She has all breeds.

*

Our daily lives betray us.

*

To love what one has is to be resigned to never getting what one wants.

*

Those who need to learn will never know a thing.

*

How many men want to be our lovers who are not worthy to be our valets.

*

What have you loved best?
—Loving.
And if you had several choices?
—I would choose love many times.

Their Lovers

She introduced me to pleasure—and I have never forgiven her.

*

How quickly one loses in their orbit everything one went there to seek.

*

Still in love: passionately performing for her things one no longer expected of oneself.

*

Loving her: having her leaps of joy.

*

Eros is the youngest of the gods—he's also the weariest.

*

How much I must love her to force myself to adopt this amorous attitude which so annoys me.

*

Lovers too should get the day off.

*

An old mistress, a kind of obscene mother.

*

Seek out those women who walk on their toes—they still exist.

*

At night, along hotel corridors, I look at the shoes before each bedroom door. The shoes of couples, down at heel, misshapen by business calls and sordid pleasures; children's shoes, personal but lacking individuality, evocative of pleasant walks, surprises and sudden, mysterious exhaustion; the shoes of well-groomed men, better-groomed...best-groomed! then the shoes of a woman alone, little tiny shoes worn down at the toe.

✳

I belonged to everyone, she belonged to no one: we considered ourselves quite different, and yet in our loneliness we were alike.

✳

We speak to each other, indeed we do, to discover we share the same silence.

✳

When you do not reply, I doubt myself, I am angry with myself, I am disloyal to myself.

✳

To wait in vain is sometimes a way of having.

✳

What is that stubborn, blinkered desire which wants only one thing? And this desire, infinitely more stubborn, infinitely more blinkered which, in that thing, wants only one thing!

✳

Only the rejection of those poor enough to inspire no other desire can make us feel aggrieved.

✳

That petty, intimate cowardice she calls her duty.

✳

Metamorphosis: the scent of jasmine with the hands of a woman.

✳

One does not give oneself to the invisible, but one can take it.

✳

Lovers? Most certainly, see how bored they are together.

✳

I waited for her and she didn't come, could I be younger than I think?

✳

They lack only time for the essentials.

✳

Gallantry refused: You gave it some importance...I should have done as you did.

✳

As others need to get drunk, I need fresh air: adieu.

*

She forgot her eyes upon my face.

*

We exchanged words which were as sweet as dreams, of which sweet nothing remains!

*

We end up preferring the leaves to the flowers.

*

Your resistance: so many sighs for the life you do not dare to live!

*

Ten yards away she was already preparing her face to smile.

*

Precious stones, a woman's lidless eyes.

*

Her eyelashes fluttered like a fan.

*

She said things which were amazed to find themselves on her lips.

*

Her hands were as warm as though all the kisses they received had come back to life.

*

I did not realize you were so tall...

—That is because I have always been on my knees before you.

*

When she lowers her eyes she seems to hold all the beauty in the world between her eyelids; when she raises them I see only myself in her gaze.

*

You are sad that she might cheat on you; she is, perhaps, the sadder.

*

Her flesh is so sensitive she feels even the shadows which prowl about her.

*

…And then to fall asleep like drunken gods.

*

I only know how to want what I want…and what I want, would you want it?

*

Violence, a pimp's argument.

*

A Russian wrote her letters like an opera libretto. Women always like reassuring cliches from those who know not to bother them with a personality in any way different from that of the usual lover. Perhaps that's their way of being faithful?

*

Courage after love: She dared to die. . . I dared to live.

*

I am leaving never to return.
—But you are looking back…
Better to appreciate that I'm leaving.

Epigrams from *Souvenirs Indiscrets*

How can we claim to possess someone else when we are scarcely in possession of ourselves.

*

In vain do jealous lovers keep watch on their beloved, she escapes them—be it only in her thoughts. Should they kill her, her escape is the more complete. How many pointless crimes are committed in this futile quest for possession?

*

Only that which changes and transforms remains alive. The tenderest of feelings is in danger of extinction if it does not evolve.
I am more passionately committed to living without illusions than to abandoning myself to them—even when they make me happy.

*

Let us try to avoid that automatism of sentiment where the same words and gestures are endlessly repeated without feeling or thought. It is that automatism which makes couples, love letters and family reunions so tedious.

*

As desire continues it becomes as monotonous as the waves: how far we are from the lightning-lit storm which fell upon us with the violence of an element unleashed.

*

A heart which does not beat with all its strength, which knows no weakness, is merely an organ.

*

How many limit their horizons to a happy life lived in harmony? Love may be fobbed off with false values; friendship requires the real thing.

*

Avoid that romantic trap: saying more than you feel, forcing your-self to feel more than you've said!

*

Light-hearted love affairs, rainbow-hued, like soap bubbles sting when the bubble bursts.

*

When we seek refuge inside ourselves, and our solitude seems pre-cious, it is because we run the risk of losing it!

*

When you're in love you never really know whether your elation comes from the qualities of the one you love, or if it attributes them to her; whether the light which surrounds her like a halo comes from you, from her, or from the meeting of your sparks.

*

"Why?" asks my beautiful, disappointing companion, "Do you care about the arts now that you have me?"

*

There are some women it would be foolhardy to take out of their natural setting: bed.

*

Every victim awaits her hour, "When I no longer care for the one who keeps me in chains, what freedom I shall have to loathe him!"

*

Often we set ourselves to love what we should only desire, then we end up marrying just anyone.

*

What makes marriage a double defeat is the fact that it works on the lowest common denominator: neither of the ill-assorted pair gets what they want.

Indiscretions

On Love

Love, that state of grace, that act of faith, to love is to take the veil.

*

Like all religions, love has more believers than practitioners.

*

Love begins where personal interest ends.

*

"Love your neighbor as yourself." It would appear that no one loves themselves.

*

Those who say their love is infinite, love infinitely little.

*

How little love there is in most love affairs!

*

If it is the most intense moments of passion we forget the soonest, that is because they are consumed by their own intensity.

*

When, after a night of love, we seek some material reminder to carry with us, it is so that we can go on believing after we've come back down to earth.

*

A grand passion is hard to bear for very long. It weighs us down, we weigh it down. Who will collapse first?

*

Loving is not as easy as it seems. To keep it alive you need a magic potion, invincible habit, or varied torment. Or perhaps all three.

*

If love needs constance and desire needs change, how can we reconcile the two?

*

What arrogance to say, "I am sure of her, I am sure of myself." Such arrogance goes before a fall.

*

In love there is no status quo.

*

Does not happiness, the well-being of the heart, like the well-being of the body, contain within it the seeds of its own destruction—starting with doubt.

*

As Renée Vivien observed, "The best part of love is friendship."

*

If passion has developed into tenderness, we should welcome that tenderness as the surest of our assets.

Alcohol

Alcohol, our common ancestor.

✳

...The only disease we drink thirstily and which is sure to destroy us— and our descendants.

✳

"God will punish you even to the third and fourth generation." Let's raise a glass of cool water to the health of the fifth generation!

✳

It was doubtless a distiller who got the superstition going that it is unlucky to drink anyone's health with water. Drinking someone's health with alcohol is a contradiction in terms.

✳

As for 'delicious wines,' is it not better to taste them than to drink them?

✳

If the wretched need their little illusions, let them have ones which will last a little longer.

✳

The exaggerations of drunkenness, false lyricism which perverts true values: I lament the enthusiasm, the writing, the friendship and love affairs which are born in ones cups.

✳

What you find in one glass you lose in the next.

✳

A man was drowned in a barrel of wine—but how many barrels of wine does each man contain?

✳

Alcohol, the vice of the blood.

Everyone would be a 'melancholy drunk' if they understood what it meant.

*

The gods need only themselves. In vain do mortals seek baneful, unworthy, intoxicating stimulants to take them out of themselves, "to get back what they're missing," as the German said!

*

One race may assimilate another, but no blood is strong enough to absorb the enemy of the human race—alcohol.

*

Having been born drunk I drink only water.

*

Brutalizing drink invades first the mind, then the guts then the generations to come.

*

Women at a dinner party become the girls they really are.... The light of dawn is too clear a mirror and they are afraid.

*

Drunk on fresh air, on night and solitude, I stretch my amorous arms toward the dawn and go home stumbling with ideas.

*

To lose one's moral health is to lose one's life, for what is a physical life worth when the mind is sick and no longer signs its own acts?

*

Lovers are not the only ones who are 'love-sick,' there are others who love their disease.

The Gods

If only original sin were original.

⁂

Only God knows how to keep his distance.

⁂

The big mistake was thinking God is good.

⁂

'The poor of heart will see God,' and the rich will be gods.

⁂

If only 'right-thinking' people could be replaced by thinking people.

⁂

Not discouraged by the mediocre quality of creation, he wants to make it eternal.

⁂

Eternity: what a waste of time.

⁂

I'm fond of human beings, but only one at a time.

⁂

Prayers tire the gods out.

⁂

It's not surprising the faithful remain adoring; they never see him.

⁂

Renouncement: the heroism of the mediocre.

⁂

The fact that experience costs us dear is probably its only redeeming feature.

⁂

Humanity is like an opera choir; it always remains in the background.

⁂

Everything serves its purpose—even goodness.

⁂

Their assertions crush many truths.

Old Age

They say it is tragic to grow old; it seems to me it would be dreadful not to know how to.

*

It is not their youth but their age they fear to lose.

*

Some women experience maturity as an incurable disease.

*

Only old age is expressive.

*

Upon her brow, a marvelous array of wrinkles in the shape of a lyre.

*

'Staying young,' trying to arrest one's development instead of evolving, keeping one's person free of personality. Faces, tell your secrets, become 'human documents' worthy of our study.

*

Her hair stayed too young for her face.

*

Her hair has gone white.
—from grief?
—from lack of henna.

*

She wears a rubber mask on her face at night!
—If only she'd wear it during the day!

*

At least the aging King David had good reason to sleep with slaves: it kept him warm.

*

I like lined faces—whose lines are well-written.

✳

Like her old parquet flooring, she was falling to pieces from being trampled on.

✳

Aged, wrinkled and scourged by the cold of too many winters.

✳

She criticized nature, who returned the compliment.

✳

Her words are so venomous they have rotted her teeth.

Theater

Sham is most easily spotted from a distance .

✳

Never trust the decor.

✳

Molière has not aged, he has just got longer.

✳

Theatre has already been supplanted by living photographs.

✳

Going into a theater I see a sign saying, "Exit," and I exit.

Literature

Novels are longer than life.

✻

The first novel, Adam and Eve's, has been overprinted.

✻

I never get to the end of an idea—it is far too far.

✻

…The stunted sensibility of those who need to watch to understand.

✻

Her hatred swarms beneath her words like wood lice beneath a stone upturned.

✻

All judgements are more or less invidious. Justice is manifold. There can be no "last judgement."

✻

Whoever speaks "against" has nothing to say. Why demolish when we can surpass? We limit ourselves to what we can attack.

✻

Even more invigorating than fighting flesh to flesh, fighting word to word.

✻

Always confiding what we have to say to a piece of paper, like the king's barber to the reeds. Does only paper have ears?

✻

Regular verse: a game of patience.

Irregular verse: a game of impatience.

*

Our memory often replaces the words of poets—and our replacements are better.

*

He accumulated a wide vocabulary and waited all his life for an idea.

*

Sacred words, short, vile and full of nonsense.

*

A thought falls like a ripe fruit from the tree of idleness.

*

Her strident voice seemed to stab the subtlety of her thoughts.

*

Do not fornicate with the minds of others: it always gives birth to a bastard.

*

Work with the ugliness life brings us, rework it in our own image.

*

So many new, bold, beautiful images sting and stimulate my imagination as I pass that instead of writing to you, I am writing to myself.

*

A good book is never exhausted; we are never exhausted by a good book.

*

Liking only the nocturnal side of life, he limited himself to masterpieces of obscurity.

*

There are also those intangible realities which float alongside us, formless and wordless, those realities which no one has put into thought, excluded for want of an interpreter.

*

The difference between what is and what could be is so slight—
Do better and worse cancel each other out?

*

Behind some writers lurks an unknown figure, often they do not
see it, not looking in the right direction; they attribute to themselves everything suggested to them by this invisible presence.

*

It is time for dead languages to keep quiet.

*

Comma: an eyelash fallen between words, the time to make a
wish, to think of something else, and to carry on.

*

When I read A. I think how much bad literature resembles good;
when I read Z I think how good literature resembles bad.

*

What makes bad writers so annoying is their good passages.

*

They are too eager to bite to be good critics.

*

They mistake a plateau for the summit.

*

He reproaches them for nit-picking, he who cannot tell nits from
wits.

*

They exult more than they exalt.

*

Genius: that excrescence.

*

Balzac: everybody; Stendahl: somebody.

*

When it comes to philosophy, let us have the courage of our indif-
ference!

*

Why does he speak so loudly? He wishes to be heard from one world to the other.

*

The arts, those accomplishments which have grown so loud we can no longer hear what it is they accomplish.

*

He preferred his friend's confessions to Jean-Jacques'.

*

I am not a bibliophile but a humanophile: I look for rare human beings.

*

It is not easy to write poetry like F…in fact it is difficult not to write poetry like F.

*

Regular verse is like dried fruit packed in a box.

*

If I blush sometimes for what I have done, it is with pure pleasure.

*

I regret neither the follies I have committed nor the follies I neglected to commit; when it comes to folly I am extremely reasonable.

*

Seeking revenge: what a lack of foresight.

Critical Sallies

To remain eternally true to eternally changing truths.

*

One's smile, one's only sincerity.

*

The romantics have appropriated all the big words, we are left with only the little ones.

*

It is harder to split hairs than steel girders.

*

Those who speak according to their lights speak for themselves; not so much that we may hear them, as to listen to themselves.

*

I am able to think my thought only after I have said it.

*

I always understand those who speak indistinctly, searching for words as they search for their ideas; theatrical voices dismay my understanding, seem to reverse the truth by their arrogant prejudice.

*

I kept quiet for fear he should realize he was not speaking to himself alone.

*

To those who ask if I have read their book, I reply: I have not yet read Homer.

*

Those who do not wound politely are mere critics.

*

Let us at least be smug about all the things we are not.

*

He used to say: one must have written a book of poems—he had written one.

*

Romanticism is a childhood ailment; those who had it young are the most robust.

*

To be rich is to introduce the unexpected even when it is required.

*

How can one fail to like the people of the Midi, they are eloquent and they are treacherous, among so many who are merely treacherous.

*

Like backward compasses, they point ever southward.

*

The worst of the up and coming is that they up and come.

*

Those who made it most recently: when will they give it back?

*

Bayreuth—what Gargantuan music—but one may not like Gargantua.

*

I noticed how he differed from those one would call his fellows, free of the exaggerations of style and costume of those for whom perversity is more attitude than instinct… A little beggar boy crossed the road, paying no attention to the traffic which was bearing down upon him: the one I had picked out took hold of him, saved his life, then wiped his hands with disgust.

*

He had the three signs of the non-entity: a receding chin, the Légion d'Honneur, a wedding ring.

*

Happy are those who keep their own counsel, they are the only ones to get any rest.

*

Every great man has a Boswell; often Boswell is the great man.

*

Your glory may depend upon one person listening to you.

*

They seem to have lived through the future.

*

How many times in the troubled reflection of a broken window pane have I seen the *chef d'oeuvre* Whistler could have painted.

*

You cut through life like a naked blade, pure and incorruptible; you are sharpened by obstacles and filth only makes you shine out more strongly. Generously you give the *coup de grace* to the dying, and from versatile minds, your fellows, you make sparks fly.

*

It is said that Mme. X...has signed her name to a painting. Why not, since she knows how to write?

*

When I first met him he still had some sensitivity, but he left that behind him in order to make it...and they call that ambition!

*

His way of being great is to be gross.

*

He's made it!
What?

*

Those who seek admiration seem to me to have little real complacency.

*

If they were only free thinkers, but they are free speakers!

*

A little man, frank enough in his frank dishonesty: well, one has to live—to live well at others' expense!

*

What low deeds to go up in the world.

*

How could I wish you ill? Are you not the worst I could have wished for you?

*

I wanted to get to meet her because of her work, but now I find her work is not big enough for me to forget her in it.

Thanks to her I know that subtlety and meanness are close in meaning; it would have been more *subtle* to leave me in ignorance.

*

We find it hard to excuse people for showing us their true face. And there was a time when I wanted that sincerity!

*

Enthusiasm propelled me, she forced me to see clearly.

*

I hesitate between disgust and pity; disgust would be more charitable.

*

I should have chosen a carnival day to look at life: the more I look at faces, the more I like masks.

*

Reduce everything to its simplest expression, then to its most complete suppression.

*

That man of fashion, from two seasons ago, with the knack of saying the right thing, late.

*

The English who pronounce the word art with a capital T.

*

I do not understand those who spend hours at the theater watching scenes between people whom they would not listen to for five minutes in real life.

*

An author I admire for the delicate order of his thoughts, laid out and labelled like beautiful captive insects, whose death enthralls us.

*

All expression, all art, is an indiscretion we commit against ourselves. This is not an 'impoverishment' but an increase in wealth, for it is in this way that we make the short hours of our lives live on beyond themselves. And discretion about our pasts, our long-gone pasts, is worthless, sterile oblivion. It is, I believe, respectful to honor our dead with a few words in which they can live again, and to give them an inspiring, courageous epitaph to what they were, instead of gradual, silent nothingness. For it is perhaps a sin to allow those prodigies to die unsung, unheard who make their own lives into their life's work. The story of their love affairs, piously gathered together, has been an ornament to the world; those are the alms their wealth affords us. It is also their only posterity. Silence too can be indiscreet. Would it not be a sign of irredeemable poverty to allow the dead to die?

*

They say, "That is a man to watch," which means he never rises above their line of vision. Very reassuring—for them.

*

All these futurists, free versifiers, destabilizers, publicity seekers and absurdists have one fault, only one, but a serious one amidst so much noisy insignificance: they throw us back on the classics with greater and greater desperation.

*

Literature is becoming quite unlivable.

*

"Every man has his price" (said an aristocrat who must have been a millionaire), but some have no commercial value—their saving grace.

*

He could do more.
—If he felt more.

*

If only art were as rare as good taste…

*

How many painters have only seen color on the palettes of others.

*

I go on…(a mistake, perhaps)

*

"I never received anything except from misers," an old courtesan once told me. Are misers the only ones with something to give?

*

That extravagance which consists of lavishing on the indifferent what we must later refuse the one we love… A worthy topic: in praise of avarice.

*

"I have nothing left," is not even an excuse.

*

Why do the poor not invent other values: would they then be truly poor?

*

The sun: the pauper's gold.

*

I never do anything silly, to leave myself room to be foolish.

*

A thin, sickly, dying mother bends over her child without shame, unabashed at letting him foresee the skeleton she has already become.

*

Not to have a beautiful mother is to start life with old age.

*

I wanted more precise information about my ancestors. I went to see my grandmother's thirteenth sister who was 102 years old, the only one still alive. She still spoke quite lucidly, and in French. Being nearly deaf and nearly blind, there was nothing to disturb her memories. She recounted insignificant details: the first to come to mind. Her mother, despite the rudimentary conditions in the United States at that time, used to file her nails with little pieces of frosted glass… Delicate habits, and an inability to adjust, brought over from France which she had left to save their fragile necks from the guillotine. Flight? As though such a death were not just compensation for necks which were too frail, stretched away from real life which they would have needed to contemplate from above… What then was this lesser bravery: exile. Cowardice? Courage? I lifted my hands to my own neck, long and frail like theirs, inordinately so, and I wished I had been born in those troubled times, which demanded absolute heroism or total cowardice, even if only to learn what blood beat most fiercely in my veins... To be caught unawares... To have a spontaneous reaction, faced with unexpected events... To escape, get outside myself, to return and know at last what I am worth before conscious reflection.

*

Democracy: the nothingness of colorless people, devoid of beauty; it is worse than ugliness.

*

It is fear of ridicule which makes all these people so ridiculous!

*

My eyes hurt. The revenge of things I have seen only too well?

*

Since nothing is impossible, nothing is inevitable.

*

We see only by contrast.

*

Lovers, those idlers who are satisfied by the first pleasures they encounter.

*

We love those whom we cannot appreciate any other way.

*

How can her friendship, satisfied with so little, satisfy me at all?

*

It is better to be a lover than to love a lover.

There are two kinds of question, the interrogative and the reply: those who ask phrase the question, those who reply shift its grounds.

*

What I like about people is the unknown and no acquaintance will ever rival it.

*

I lost sight of her, or rather she lost sight of me: how many people we see only in profile!

*

It is hard to forgive a sensual being for liking neither vice nor debauchery.

*

It is dangerous to look down upon things from above, unless one was born on top of them.

*

Perhaps you are right, but perhaps being right is not such a big thing.

*

That parasite: the past.

*

How many yesterdays there are in tomorrow!

*

You should not fear to survive the dead, but your own self.

*

My voice is low, so that only I may hear?

*

You gain nothing by questioning a singer.

*

A waterfall, made smaller by distance, is framed by my window. Light and youthful as a lock of hair, it flows. Not falling in a straight line, it does not reach its full length, being continually intercepted by the strong wind. Unfaithful, away it flies, before it can touch the rock it has wet (and which at other times it shapes, uses and transforms,) to join that passing force which carries it off, light as air, and which, being freer, outlasts it.

*

Love, like Ben Johnson's goose: too big for one, too small for two!

*

A face wondrously chiselled by emotion. Each line told of some former joy. I compared it with those other faces ruined by old age and habit, upon which time had left but one sign: destruction.

*

What diversity amongst the ruins!

*

Grace, power grown civil.

*

The finest life is spent creating oneself, not procreating.

*

Perhaps it is our belief in fate which makes it fateful.

*

Why resuscitate old gods when new gods are waiting to be created?

*

A god who is not also a devil, what an incomplete being!

*

Love, what a work of juvenilia!

*

I find it difficult to believe there are as many nights as there are days.
Certain seeds are scattered here, but what of the uncertain ones:
less colorless, taking wing?

*

Observing oneself is dangerous—but not observing oneself is boring.

*

One looks differently into a mirror.

*

Many of my thoughts belonged to others before me (I blush only
with pride in my predecessors), many will be adopted by others
after I have gone... Repeating something true does not make it
less true, except perhaps for he who said it before!

*

That most difficult of accomplishments—oneself.

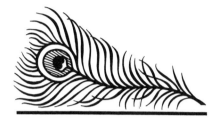

Part Five: Friends From the Left Bank

The Colette I Knew

The dead belong to us more than the living, for they force us to gather together the inheritance of memories they bequeath us, from which to get our bearings, and make a final tally—draw out the essence of countless hours spent together, in which we find ourselves all too often replaced by a mere semblance.

Beyond these encounters, in which Colette excelled at playing Colette, what was our relationship really like, apart from that lazy intimacy where we would often see but misread each other?

Did I experience with Colette any of those flashes of recognition in which the mysterious nature of another being is suddenly revealed? But perhaps an affectionate friendship such as ours had no need of violent revelation.

In contrast to the fluctuations of love, the constancy of such a sentiment was a haven, sheltering us from the storms by which we were all too often assailed.

The English saying, "Love me little, love me long," has some truth in it, but how can we apply a coat of varnish to the comforting images of the past, now grown a little dim, and make them sharper?

For a start, here are some lines from Colette's *Claudine s'en va,* come to my aid, highlighting the vivid colors and certain aspects of our childhoods:

> Miss Flossie, declining a cup of tea, gives voice to such an elongated "no," in her throaty little drawl, that she seems in total agreement with herself. Alain does not want me (why?) to get to know this American, more supple than a scarf, whose glowing face shimmers with golden hair, sea blue eyes and implacable teeth. She smiles easily at me, her eyes fixed on

mine, until a peculiar quiver of her left eyebrow, as troubling as a call for help, makes me look away... Miss Flossie smiles more nervously this time, while a slim red-headed child, crouching in her shadow, gazes intently at me with deep, hate-filled eyes...

Was I really that greedy, wasteful Flossie?[1] I do not know, but already aware of true values and lasting friendship, I have never lost sight of Colette for long. So the times we spent together come back in waves. How can I choose amongst them? I jot some down at random. At the beginning of our century, when I first saw Colette, she was no longer the slim adolescent with long braids lying in the hammock, but a young woman solidly planted on her stocky legs, her back swaying out to a rounded behind; her manners were as frank as her language, but her enigmatic, triangular face had a feline silence about it, and her beautiful grey eyes with their eyebrows slit lengthwise, held a slow trickling glance which had no need to make itself seductive in order to seduce.

Her favorite companions, a cat and a dog—as everyone knows—were doubtless chosen for their singular resemblance to their mistress. Was not her nature a combination of these two animals? Obedient and devoted to one master, while secretly enjoying the instincts of the feral beast which escapes all domination.

Dressed in button-up boots for long walks, she would take her animals to the *Bois*, beyond the *Sentier de la vertu* where ladies of "little virtue" merely climbed out of their carriages and took a few steps—to which they give the ridiculous name of "footing"—their perfume blending with that of the acacias which fell at their feet in little showers of blossom, to be crushed under high heel shoes. Liane de Pougy, driving amongst her rivals, fascinated me by her androgynous slenderness, setting her apart from those who cultivated plumpness as an irresistibly feminine attribute.

"In the age of horse-drawn carriages" one had time to exchange long glances and half smiles as one drove from the *Tir aux pigeons [Shooting Gallery]* to the *Cascade [Waterfall]*, passing and repassing most of the courtesans, actresses, society ladies and demimondaines of the day.

---

1. The name given to Miss Barney in Liane de Pougy's *Idylle Saphique.*

None had, we felt, a smile as beautiful as Colette's.

I met the Willys at the home of the Countess Armande de Chabannes, and they invited me to their house in the Rue de Courcelles. I was particularly intrigued by the little gymnasium they had in their apartment, for back in the United States we ran in the fresh air, rode horses, played tennis, rowed on Frenchman's Bay in Bar Harbour, never dreaming that these sports could be the subject of methodical training.

Colette practiced regularly on the barre, the trapeze, the rings—for a future music-hall act, perhaps. But the other workroom, in which the schoolgirl learned to write novels under Willy's tutelage, remained invisible. Was it perhaps their bedroom, serving a dual purpose?

This couple, who denied themselves the luxury of a private life, were seen everywhere together and soon, considering the art of publicity as the surest aid to the writer's craft, Willy enlarged the picture by annexing Mademoiselle Polaire to the couple.

He forced not only Colette but also Polaire to cut her hair[2] and go dressed as "Claudine at School" twins the better to illustrate those schoolgirl passions—which neither Colette nor Polaire felt for each other. That this cultured individual, who was also a man of letters and the most influential music critic of the time,[3] should stoop to amuse himself in this role is all the more surprising given that in those days people were still quite fearful of compromising themselves by scandal. It took a certain courage to provoke a scandal like that and turn it to one's own benefit for, even nowadays, it is not within everyone's capabilities to create a bad reputation for themselves.

Another characteristic of that master publicist was revealed to me by his vigilant supervision of his wife's comings and goings, despite his good nature, or pretended good nature. He watched her closely, less out of love than the desire to curtail anything

---

2. "Lucie Delarue Mardrus also cut her flowing brown hair, the massive tresses she had worn wrapped around her head for so long. My own hair, measuring six foot three inches, the silver thatch which crowned the forehead of the Amazon, what a harvest cut down by the whim of fashion!" (*L'Etoile vesper*)
3. Author of a daring music paper published under the name of *L'Ouvreuse [The Usherette]* to which Colette contributed.

which did not serve to pleasure or profit that odd ménage à trois. Willy was kind enough to lend me Colette, without Polaire, to play in a pastoral scene which she later described as follows:

One fine afternoon on a lawn in Neuilly, in Miss Natalie C-B's garden, I performed Pierre Loüys' *Dialogue au soleil couchant* *[Dialogue at the setting of the sun]*. The other impromptu actress was called Eva Palmer, a miraculous redhead with hair down to her feet. Only on my elder half-sister have I seen such abundance as graced Eva's forehead. For our Dialogue she had twisted this exceptional adornment into long ropes and put on a Greek-looking tunic of greeny-blue, while I considered myself a perfect Daphnis by virtue of a very short piece of terra cotta crêpe de chine, a Roman buskin and a crown borrowed from Tahiti.

Eva Palmer, very pale, stammered out her part. The rolled Rs of my native Burgundy accent became Russian with stage fright. Pierre Loüys, one of the guests, listened. Perhaps he did not listen, for the sight of us was sweeter than the sound. But we believed that Paris, under its parasols and the enormous hats fashionable that year, thought only of us... Afterwards grown bolder, I dared ask Loüys whether "it had not gone too badly."

"I have just experienced the strongest emotion of my life."

"Oh! dear Loüys."

"I assure you. The unforgettable impression of hearing my work performed by Mark Twain and Tolstoy."

Eva Palmer blushed red under the red crown of braids twined and intertwined across her forehead and Pierre Loüys added some consoling remark, joining Natalie Barney and friends in their kind praise. But suddenly all attention was diverted from the Boston shepherdess and the Moscow shepherd by a naked woman on a white horse with a harness of turquoises who was making her entrance from the wings of greenery, a dancer whose unfamiliar name had already achieved some renown amongst the salons, sets and studios: Mata-Hari.

Under the May sun of Neuilly, despite the turquoises, the loose black mane, the tinsel diadem and, especially, the long thigh against the white flank of the Arab stallion, what was surprising was the color of her skin, not brown and succulent as under the lights, but an uneven, artificial purplish-blue. Once the horse parade was over she dismounted and covered herself with a sari. She greeted people, talked, was a little disappointing... It was even worse when Miss Barney invited her, as a private individual, to a second garden party.

—*Mes apprentissages [My Apprentiship]*

It became instead a closed gathering. And this time I had a distressing example of the constraint to which Willy subjected Colette: when I arrived at their house to invite Colette alone to the hastily improvised little party I was preparing at my house in Neuilly, at which Mata-Hari had offered to give another performance of her Javanese dances, but naked this time and for a group of ladies only, Willy, bad-tempered at being thus excluded, would not give his permission unless he could impose indecent conditions. And on the way Colette confessed, "I am ashamed that you have seen my chain so close up."

The chain served, nonetheless, to discipline her gifts as a writer and Willy, that idle, perverse man of letters, proved himself a better teacher of the art of writing than the art of love.

I was called home at that point, to my family in the United States, so I am not sure when or how Colette finally freed herself of her manager, Willy, so that she could live, love and write under her own name and in her own way.

Would Colette have got divorced under other circumstances? I do not believe so, for being married and living with the person of her choice was more in keeping with her temperament than regaining her freedom, only to ask herself over and over, "What to do with it?"

Is this not clearly seen in her books, *Mes apprentissages* and *La Retraite sentimentale*?

Torn between the contradictory desires of her dual nature: to have a master and not to have one, she always chose the first solution, for Colette, though rich in herself, found it hard to live alone.

As for me, if I may slip a personal remark into these memories:

living alone and my own master is essential, not through egotism
or lack of love but the better to attend to others. Whereas drown-
ing a passionate intimacy in daily life, living together in the same
house, often in the same bedroom as the beloved, has always
seemed to me the surest way to lose her.

Moreover, does not that dreadful word "collage" [stuck like
glue; living in sin] contain a warning of sorts? To be "stuck
together", to the point where you no longer see each other, is that
a desirable goal for a relationship?

Is there not a middle ground between the two extremes of the
song:

> You are the woman who is desired
> Between two mornings and two evenings
> Unless you can be held for life entire.

And in the latter case, what tact one needs to display to renew
oneself while keeping the chosen object "for life entire."

Colette, who followed the instincts of a tiger-kitten, would
either love or hate her partners overmuch and was in danger of
suffocating them by her possessiveness.

When she had to separate from her two husbands, because of
their infidelity or their despotism, she began to hate them in direct
proportion to the amount she had previously loved them. Beast of
prey and submission, transformed into a praying mantis, she mas-
sacred them.

Does not love, tested in this way, have too much in common
with the animal kingdom?

Profiting from this experience and the demands of my own
nature—if I may continue my confession—I believe I resolved the
problem in the following way, although it is not within the natural or material capabilities of all lovers:

Two houses joined by a common garden and—essential ingre-
dient—two street doors

Thoroughly taken with this idea, I had discovered a well-
timbered property with fountains and outbuildings at Neuilly, just
opposite the Ile de Puteaux, and rented it on the spot. I moved
into the single storey house and put the maisonette at the disposal

of friends who were living, or staying, in Paris. And it was there that I lived most happily.

Colette, who was part of a group of artists,including Sacha Guitry and Marguerite Moréno (to whom she remained a loyal friend), would often visit me there. And since I had just finished a play based on Sappho's fragments, the group lent me their assistance, as did Raymond Duncan's Greek wife, "Penelope," who had just arrived from Athens with her flute, on which she would play Ionian airs. All this (despite the lorgnette hanging from Lyses' peplum, a lorgnette from which she refused to be parted) created the right atmosphere for my two verse acts to be greatly appreciated, even by those guests who were most resistant to classical poetry—including Colette herself who, though she never admitted it, could only tolerate the free verse that is born of prose, the kind of poetry which embues her own books with so much art and nature.

Amazon, there is no serenity crueller than yours.

I marvel not at your persistent, youthful, biting wit, but at the serenity which falls upon us from on high.

Just enough love. Just enough scorn for love.

Too bad for those who are not enlightened about friendship, as you and I are.

You have no idea how shy the word "pensées" has always made me. I would never have dared express myself in "pensées". I do not think enough. Fine material for a writer, a thought with nothing to clothe it!

To my knowledge only two poetesses gained Colette's approbation: her friend Hélène Picard and, most recently, Lucienne Desnoues, "because she is so fond of trees" and because her poem on the elm disease struck a sensitive cord in Colette. She asked me to send her *Le Jardin délivré* [The Rescued Garden] by that poetess, a little collection which won my Renée-Vivien prize in 1952.

As for Renée Vivien's poetry, and Renée Vivien herself, were they dear to her? Not according to *Ces plaisirs*, in which Colette judges her without understanding or consideration.

Certainly, Colette disliked that kind of poetry, although she agreed to mime *Le Faune,* which Renée Vivien had dedicated to her—in my woodland this time. Poetesses who were closer to nature, like Lucie Delarue-Mardrus, should have pleased her better, and yet the Norman and the Burgundian, despite a pretence at friendship, were not fond of each other. Madame Mardrus complained, quite rightly, that she was "sandwiched between Colette's novels and Anna de Noailles' poetry." It must have been hard for Colette to speak in praise of Anna de Noailles—with simulated emotion—when she replaced her at the Belgian Academy. Glory has its own tyranny!

As for Germaine de Beaumont, that inexhaustible spring bubbling with poetry, who was and remains her fervent disciple and great friend, I wonder whether Colette appreciated her true worth. In any case, no one cherished her or served and sang her praises better than that novelist and poet, and that from the first hour to her last.

But let us follow Colette in that period when she was obliged to return to the music-hall. The scenes in which she appeared were less provocative and she was better prepared (by her partner and teacher, Georges Wague). And this time she succeeded in pleasing the public.

During her years of wandering, Colette performed once more at my house, not as a mime but as an actress, as well as at my salon in Paris in the Rue Jacob. Colette, predestined to return to that old garden, describes it as follows in *Trois, six, neuf [Three, six, nine]:*

> Most of the houses which line the Rue Jacob, between the Rue Bonaparte and the Rue de Seine, date from the eighteenth century. The only danger I faced in the Rue Jacob was the lure of the shadows, the brief gusts of fresh air, a few blasts of spring hail shot through the open window, the vague smell of some invisible lilac coming from the garden next-door.
> Leaning a long way over the window sill, all I managed to glimpse of that garden was the top of a tree. I did not know that this den of rustling leaves signalled the favorite haunt of

Rémy de Gourmont and the garden of his "amazone." Much later I was to go beyond the garden fence and visit the little temple which Adrienne Lecouvreur had built "to friendship." Hidden from the sun, even today that garden will only nurture a graveyard ivy, frail and aged trees and those aqueous plants which grow in wreaths on the inside of wells.

It was in my salon, between the courtyard and the garden that she presented the first performance of her play: *La Vagabonde*, which was later performed in the theatre with Paul Poiret, achieving the limelight in a single season.

Were Poiret and Colette too creative in their other roles to succeed as actor and actress? I do not know, but Colette did not excel, even when she played Léa in her *Chéri*.

Who would have the luck to stop Colette, launched like Atalanta, but on the wrong road? Another runner whom she met on the way, in good training, and with many an easy victory under his belt.

Does not Colette relate in her novel, *L'Entrave*, by what irresistible attraction, the partners in a foursome race found themselves swopped round on the way?

Did Colette realize, good sport that she was, that the high stakes she was playing for would be too taxing for that gallant, who later offered, gallantly, to marry her? It was not without apprehension that I saw Colette married to Henri de Jouvenel, settling down bravely and lovingly in a real marriage with a fine husband, baby, nanny, servants, etc... Despite many shared tastes, including food and bed, despite the interests which united them in their dual employment at *Le Matin* newspaper, there was nothing to reassure me that this union, which seemed happy enough, was going to last. There must be perfectly happy, united marriages, but why are they never those one knows? Moreover, how could that tall dark-haired man, in the flower of youth, intelligent and vain, beloved of women—and who loved women—be tied down to just one, even if it were Colette—a Colette who, moreover, offered not only all her love, but the originality of her mind and a whole new environment?

It was in her office at *Le Matin* that I witnessed one of the first
marital scenes between that couple in which Colette, despite her
instinctive vigilance, had let herself go so far as to blossom with
happiness.

That evening, having finished her journalistic work, Colette
was still sitting at her table and we were having a tête-à-tête, when
"Henry" came in, apparently in great good humor, and after greet-
ing me in a friendly way, turned to Colette in a free and easy tone,
full of complacency:

"Please do not wait dinner for me tonight."

"But," said Colette, disconcerted, "you will be home soon
afterward?"

Jouvenel, who was standing behind Colette's chair, glanced at
me as he replied to this question—for he did not seem put out at
having a witness for his first declaration of independence, "No, I
am afraid it will be quite late. Do not wait up for me."

The blow struck home and Jouvenel was pleased to have
shown how important he was to her. Faced with Colette's distracted silence, he derived pleasure from her suffering, superior as
she was to him in every way, especially in love.

What was more natural than that Jouvenel, during this test of
his fidelity, should tire in the end of being deprived of a change in
his female diet, not only due to his male vanity but also his vora-
cious sensuality? But Colette, who was tenacious and exclusive,
did not see it like that and having been similarly deserted on several other occasions, her revenge was not long in coming. Outraged, more from pride than love, Henri de Jouvenel retreated to
his mother's, waiting for the divorce to be announced.

Despite her brave swagger, it was awhile before Colette was
herself again. She made friends with one of her ex-rivals, the better
to loathe the unfaithful husband. This flash of temperament
inspired her novel *La seconde*, which has recently been made into a
play.

Her daughter's growing resemblance to the despised husband
was probably a trial to Colette's maternal feelings. She brought her
daughter up with the greatest care nonetheless just as her mother,
Sido, had brought her up, with shrewd rather than close attention.

For was it not important to give the child, whom she enjoyed watching grow, the chance to develop in her own way? Having fulfilled her duty, Colette, like the cat "Nonoche," answered the call of her nature once again.

Meanwhile her daughter "Belgazou," who was only just of age, threw herself away in a marriage whose only possible outcome was a separation followed by divorce.

Freed from this first experiment, the only result of which was to discourage her from marriage altogether, Belgazou, having acquired her own "look" under the Saint Tropez sun, her pretty bronzed skin contrasting with her sunbleached platinum blonde hair, attracted the attention and admiration of the painter, Kisling, who did her portrait.

Imagine my surprise, as I strolled along the pier in Saint Tropez one evening, upon seeing "Belgazou" scarcely recognizable beneath layers of make-up of rabble-pink and bruise-blue, badly applied to her young eyelids and her pretty cheeks with their high cheekbones. That make-up made her look more like a call-girl than the rather fierce young woman she was. I learned that this attempt at embellishment came courtesy of Colette's maternal hands—still far from expert at her new trade of aesthetician which she plied in a little beauty salon run by her best friend Maurice Goudeket.

Cécile Sorel, wanting to be helpful, offered herself as a model but as Colette changed method from one eye to another the result was an asymmetry which doubled the great actress's age and discouraged other volunteers.

Colette obstinately continued and, after several further attempts on more innocent victims recruited from her immediate circle, agreed to do a make-up demonstration in one of the big Parisian stores. The results of the demonstration were not encouraging and Colette abandoned the profession, for which she had shown more perseverance than talent, to continue her writing in her villa, *La Treille Muscate*. It was there that she composed the finest pages of *La Naissance du Jour*.

Maurice Goudeket, now established in her life, dedicated himself to her entirely, deserving his later title: "the best of her three husbands."

Maurice tirelessly responded to her smallest desire and lavished her with staunch devotion. I became aware of his devoted attention one evening when we were dining with some neighbors, the dog, Tobie, sitting beside us.

Despite her "conviviality," Colette, who was always very attentive to her pets, noticed that her little black ball was beginning to get sick and, by that telepathy which reigns in well-assorted couples, communicated her apprehension to Maurice who immediately went to get a large travelling-rug from the car in which he wrapped the dog and carried her off.

The dog, who was indeed in the state Colette suspected, let herself be taken away but not without gazing at her mistress, over Maurice's shoulder, with the expression of a weeping negress.

Colette had often had less domesticated pets in the past, like her squirrel and her cats, but in the end preferred the dog which displayed total adoration and submission.

Colette began to realize the importance her personality had acquired and the growing influence she had over her circle. So with her joyous sense of authority, she became the leader of a whole group of friends. Her gluttony, well-known and applauded, was apparent wherever she went: I can see Colette now in the back of a shop full of vats of olive oil, lifting off the lid of one, dipping her finger in to taste the oil and check it had ripened to her taste.

I see her again, sunny as always, stopping beside the Mediterranean and exclaiming:

"How solid that blue looks, why you could build on it!"

I see her one night on our terrace at Beauvallon, looking at a new moon whose transparent slenderness we were admiring. One of us, indulging in an exaggerated lyricism, was brought back to earth by Colette:

"Oh really, that moon looks like a nail clipping, pure and simple."

And, before our rapture at the smell of a gardenia,

"What a fuss! It smells like a mushroom."

She lived contentedly, reconciled with the truth of things, saved from misleading illusions, allowing herself to be naturally and fulsomely happy.

I see her in the summer at Saint Tropez, in her flesh-colored house, with its terraces inviting one to doze all night long in the open air. The house, with its garden running alongside the road to the beach by the great salt marsh, was hidden by so many flowers and vegetables all growing together that one could scarcely see the door; the back of the house overlooked a creek where one could bathe unobserved.

One morning, she invited me to go for a swim with her; I reproached her for treading water without making any progress.

"But where do you want me to go?" she exclaimed.

Her heart and her senses were satisfied by Maurice, and her "Pauline" was already looking after her and taking care of all domestic concerns, so she could throw herself into her work. When she wanted to relax, she was surrounded by kind and adoring neighbors. Her daughter played not far away with friends her own age, while old friends, knowing she had settled there, would visit her when they were passing through, to pay their respects and bring her the little offerings owed to recognized divinities.

Colette enjoyed the freedom of Saint Tropez. After she had cut some superfluous embellishments from *Duo*, the novel she had just finished, Géraldy suggested that he turn it into a play. He told her that in order for it to work in the theatre she would need to add a third act and bring the third character out of the shadows. She cut him short, "I've done my work. Now you do yours." Which he did, and it took him nearly two years since he had to transpose the setting and the characters... When he returned at last to *La Treille Muscate* with the finished manuscript, Colette greeted him, "Come here and let me nitpick." Resistant and stubborn to begin with, in the end she approved of the changes.

"I was only unfaithful to it," explained Geraldy doggedly, "to be more faithful in the end."

Having finished reading the play, Colette hugged him and said, "It's fun working with you."

Duo, the result of that collaboration, played in three theaters and twenty years later it is still playing at the Théâtre Français.

When *Gigi* was published, Géraldy impressed upon Colette how successful the story would be on the stage. Once again, his prophecy held good.

Dear charming Géraldy, most attentive of friends! His eagerness to be of help to his fellows is unequalled, except, taking
myself as example, by their abuse of it! He tolerates men's character defects with less indulgence than the more touching faults of
women, whom he treats as surprising little divinities who reveal
the mysterious instincts of the eternal feminine. This moved me
to say, "Géraldy, you are too subtle, too full of nuance for the love
of a woman, for that hard struggle."

All this made those years the most beneficial of Colette's life.

The bitter crease in which her smile ended so delicately bore
witness to her hard experiences, but afterwards did not Colette at
last hold her life in her own strong hands, as well as a very successful vocation which, though it gave her much trouble, brought her
admiration, love, friendship, ease and glory.

But fate does not allow bliss to last too long: overconfident, she
lost her footing at dusk in a rut hollowed out by the heavy carts of
the grape-pickers. It gave her a sprained ankle and put her hip out
of joint; little by little arthritis set in and pain with it.

The war of 1939 brought more trials. To that major catas-
trophe with its procession of perils and restrictions of all kinds,
was added the incarceration of Maurice, who was of Jewish
descent. She had to pull out all the stops in order to save him, and
succeeded thanks to friends in high places both in France and
abroad. But the anguish sapped her strength so much that when
she caught sight of herself in the mirror she was unable to recognize herself in the distorted face reflected in the glass.

Nothing ages one faster than that kind of anxiety, the ordeal of
two wars left us all more or less afflicted.

Here are two letters that Colette wrote to me a little after the
end of hostilities:

5th December 1946

Oh foster-mother! Everything you send is useful and pleasant
in different ways! I am bothered by one scruple, just one: aren't
you depriving someone else for my benefit? This morning you
would have recognized in me the old cat, inebriated not only by
the contents but also by the container. I decided a long time

ago, what's more, to learn English only from the "Instructions for Use" printed on tins. What double joy, I had just read in that morning's paper: "The American parcels have been suspended."

But come and see me. My door and my arms are always open to you. Your calm face, have I ever loved it more? I am waiting for you. If the zealous Pauline wants to protect my rest (which she disturbs better than anyone), do not listen to her but come on in. I embrace you tenderly.

Maurice sends his warmest regards.   —Colette

18th January 1950

My very dear friend,

Berthe was kind enough to let me choose among three photos of you. I picked the tandem, in which you have two little golden tufts on either side of your bowler hat. Two horses for one amazon! What strange customs!

I am glad to know that fine weather follows you. I would also like it if some unexpected chance allowed me to take a holiday in the same area as you for once. In my daily life I am so silent and motionless that you would scarcely notice my presence. As for Maurice, I believe he is the pearl, the jewel of country neighbors. Present or absent just when one wants. I should have adopted that man twenty years earlier...but then we would have caused a scandal—perhaps. Write to me again, if you can. Is Lily still in a turmoil over the same person? Give her, and Romaine, all my love...   —Colette

My reply:

1st February, 1950

Hôtel Bristol
Beaulieu-sur-Mer

My dearest Colette,

Fine weather is with me no longer... Yes, do let's find a sheltered place for our holidays where I can see you in a long, lazy way—in slow-motion! I am relieved that you can preside over the Prix Goncourt, unless like Anderson's little mermaid, each step causes you sharp pain—which does not affect "the diversion of the mind," as you put it with a fortitude it would be vain to wish to see reduced!

Pain did not stop Colette and she went back to her desk and set to work, sitting on the chaise-longue in her apartment overlooking the Palais-Royal where she wrote, *Paris de ma fenêtre.* Other books followed, but they were punctuated with melancholy, like the arrival of the meadow saffron casting their mauve mourning over the meadows at the end of summer.

Her *Fanal bleu,* which was joined by *Etoile Vesper,* shone with subdued but faithful brilliance, first at her window, then on the bookshop shelves.

I can still hear the confident voice in which she would call and tirelessly repeat, "Maurice"—rolling the r of his name to make it last longer, certain that each time she would be supported or assisted by her best friend—in that well modulated voice which would become imperious or imploring when a decision presented itself, or an over-long visit exacerbated the pain she was in.

She strove valiantly to get the better of the pain, which came and went, impatient for periods of remission and, with a rare courage, refusing the tranquilizers which would have had a pernicious effect on her work and vitality. The pain, which was incurable, might have overwhelmed Colette if death had not put an end to it, and terminated a life which had already accorded her everything, even that easy death which gathered her up before she was aware of its presence.

But since the precious, life-giving habit of going to see Colette had been taken from me, with what could I replace it?

Worshipping neither funerals nor graveyards, I consider it a wasted exercise to try to draw near a body whose spirit has already abandoned it.

I have always found it indiscreet to watch the living sleep, how much more so to contemplate the dead.

It is customary to believe, as one prays on their graves, that they are at rest in the depths of their last sleep from which only the trumpet of the Last Judgement will awaken them.

Having endured that long drawn-out ordeal, while still fulfilling her duty as a writer without shirking, there was nothing

Colette needed to be forgiven. Ignorant of sin, and of both the heaven and the hell of believers, she must be sleeping in peace, blending into the nature she loved. Nature, cruel and beautiful as a religion, which she had followed and served with such vigor.

And what need had she of dogma or confessor, she who made her confession an open book, open to the sky, who bore the harsh discipline of life without complaint?

To those who criticize her for having debased love to the level of sensuality, came the excellent reply that on the contrary, she had raised sensuality to the level of love, a love evidently free of mysticism. Spirituality not being her strong point, Colette's talent was limited to her senses—which were possessed of prodigious antennae.

Some critics have reproached Colette for her "too narrow vision." But can one scold someone for their shortsightedness especially when, like a sort of natural microscope, they are able to appreciate the fine detail they observe close up better than anyone? Furthermore, the other senses become more acute by way of compensation.

While normal vision blurs with old age, when one so nearsighted looks into the distance, she recreates an atmosphere.

The days of diminishment arrive, at first one renounces the horizon for the sake of the landscape, then the landscape for a garden; then, confined to the house, one ends up confined to bed—where each day takes away a little courage and strength.

Reduced thus to her chaise-longue, Colette retires within herself where she painstakingly gathers up what she has seen and the things that have happened to her. She remembers with the accuracy of a prisoner confined to four walls who is able to recreate all that escapes our overstimulated senses.

She captured these essences so well that she condenses and offers them to us in each of her books, in such a personal style that as we read we seem to breathe her in, whole and entire.

As I have written elsewhere (*Aventures de l'esprit*, 1929) "Colette likes what is, and draws comfort from the earth, that wholesome dish. If, enjoying life enough to get along without eternity, she sometimes allows her soul a flight, she rarely flies higher than her own nest."

And what treasures she had laid in that series of nests! Books which are ours to read and re-read, with more attention than when she was alive. When she was alive, when we always thought there was time enough. Now, among so many tokens of the past, under such a pallid sky, where are those "momentary flashes" to help me show what she was like?—in the same gripping way as a familiar landscape which has never been seen before in the same light. Must I await that revelation? Meanwhile, I can describe her as she was each time I went to see her; I had only to lower my eyelids as I approached the better to breathe her atmosphere. Leaving other visitors to kiss her cheek, I bent over her hair—that misty aromatic cloud—as though coming closer to what she was thinking. And while her other friends listened to that sensual voice, I felt I could hear everything she did not say. Was it not from that head, as from a bushy, deep-rooted plant, that her writing blossomed? In her absence, can I not find her again the more surely now in her writing?

Rémy de Gourmont
How I Became His Amazon

How could one approach the hermit of the Rue des Saints-Pères, that monk of the mind in his gown of sackcloth, living alone in his cell of books, above everything and everyone? It was my neighbor, Edouard Champion, who provided the opportunity. Moved by the poems I had written on the death of Renée Vivien, he wanted to show them to Gourmont who decided in turn to publish them in a forthcoming issue of the *Mercure de France.*

I sent him a thank you note slipped inside *Eparpillements*, my book of epigrams. He replied immediately,

23rd June 1910

Dear Mademoiselle,

Your subterfuge nearly worked. I open, cut and read your *Eparpillements* without seeing the letter on the first two leaves. Only the brief dedication struck my eye. It was not until I re-read the book, which I enjoyed, that I found that which makes it dearer yet. It is a great thing to have charmed you, and to receive recognition of that fact: I appreciate the value of those leaves, they are precious to me.

In the printed pages which follow I discovered a noble and delicate spirit (and much else besides) with whom I feel in sympathy, even when it seems enigmatic. But one should remain an enigma, even to oneself.

After this epistolary beginning, Edouard Champion suggested that I accompany him to Rémy de Gourmont's "day"—to which he invited only a few literary persons or close friends: Apollinaire and Rouveyre. But a female stranger?

"Not such a stranger, since he knows and likes your poems and epigrams."

Rémy de Gourmont opened the door, stood straight in front of me and held out his hand warmly. I was nervous and hardly noticed his scarred face and swollen lips but stammered out something or other, for my attention was caught by his pale eyes which changed with each thought that struck him. There was a spontaneity in his welcome, a hesitancy in his demeanor and a repressed *joie de vivre* in his gaze.

How could I set that joy free? Persuade him to mix once more with the living? There was such a gap between the cloistered life he led among his books and writing and real life! With the exception of an occasional flight towards Rouen, he went out on routine business only: from the *Mercure de France* to the *Revue des Idées*, from the bookstalls of the Quai Voltaire to the Café du Flore.

This encounter with Rémy de Gourmont, without demands on either side, left us free to see each other again or not.

Our first meeting, far from putting a full stop to our correspondence was, on the contrary, only the beginning.

During another visit I had the temerity to suggest a ride to the *Bois* one afternoon in the near future. Not knowing how to refuse, he grumbled that "he did not..."

I interrupted, "Yes, yes, I'll come and fetch you. Sometimes one needs to rebel against one's habits; even if only to return to them with renewed pleasure."

My chauffeur went to fetch him at the appointed hour. Gourmont climbed into my Renault without too much trouble, despite its wide running board, and sat down next to me without saying a word. How to interrupt this silence? To a mind which is sufficient unto itself, nothing seems worth the trouble of being put into words. I kept quiet too, to give him time to get over whatever he must be feeling upon finding himself travelling toward the Bois de Boulogne away from his usual haunts. The *Bois* greeted us with the scent of its acacias. Rémy de Gourmont, despite his grumbling, could not resist sniffing the air. We stopped beside the great lake; as he gazed at one last shimmer on the water he gave a sigh.

How could one remain unaffected by the beauty of the hour and the place? He shrugged it off, saying that, like Mérimée, were he to see diamonds sparkling on the ground, he would not even stoop to pick them up, having no one to give them to.

"Nor I," I said sadly.

His face brightened at last, with a quick glance at me, he rejoined, "Do not forget that I know your poems and epigrams."

"They were for a dead woman."

"Not all."

I do not remember what else we said. What a long and difficult conquest is that of a person's mind! But his was worth all my patience and all my prudence. I had learned patience with Renée Vivien, if not prudence.

Setting aside the problem for a moment, I left for Evian with someone who was equally difficult to captivate, for other reasons, and who seemed equally worth the trouble. I was agreeably surprised to receive this unexpected letter from Rémy de Gourmont near the beginning of my stay:

Paris, 20th August 1910

My resentment, already nearly a week old, has turned against me, seeing that I would do nothing to spur it on. I am certainly not in the habit of walking in the evening with young women in the Bois de Boulogne, so I did not begin to enjoy the situation until after it was over. Not because it was unpleasant, but rather because it was too pleasant and because it presupposed a state of mind I had no reason to believe was your own. And anyway the moon over the Bois is too much like an electric light bulb. I found you terribly intimidating though your voice was soft and natural. Perhaps that is what threw me off guard, your naturalness, though I expected nothing else from you. But since it is very rare for a woman to be natural, one needs to be prepared.

That long, short walk will remain in my memory just as it was, when I had no other prompting but to listen to your voice like ironic music (the irony was mine, against myself).

Now something tells me I may have found a friend with whom to play at life again from time to time, when you have the time to spare?

Goodbye. You are in Evian. Drink the water. It is very good.

What a responsibility it is to become part of someone's life! Did I have the right? Should I run the risk of disturbing my new friend with hope and expectations? Had he not recently replied to a woman who was infatuated with his writing and who had asked to meet him, that: "There was not even room in his life for a hairpin."

As a true friend I had to think of him first, rather than myself. I was certainly attracted by the vigor and diversity of his books, the freedom of his opinions (one of which had lost him his job at the Bibliothèque Nationale and was the motivation for his joining the *Mercure de France*). I felt a sense of kinship with that most well-balanced, most learned, sincerest mind of our time, whose calibre has been attested by others more competent to judge than I. For Henri de Régnier, "He is our Montaigne, he is our Sainte-Beuve, he is our Gourmont." Léautaud himself remarked in his *Journal*, "There is no writer to equal de Gourmont in modern times."

What gift could I bring that Latin Celt, the best of the writer philosophers and philosopher writers, dedicated to "eternal parchments" and so rich in himself? Let him experience a little of the life of which he had been too soon deprived? Did I respond to the appeal I had provoked? I no longer know, but a letter of his dated 4th October shows that I saw him again and suggested I come to his next "day." An arrangement for a box to watch Molière having fallen through, he wrote to me:

Would you like me to come on Wednesday, around 5 o'clock and take a turn or two in your garden? We have already had a Wednesday... Sunday in any case. And of course I expect you as usual. Say as I do.

—Your friend, Rémy.

I would sometimes accompany him on his usual round to the Gare d'Orsay where he delivered his article for *La Dépêche de Toulouse.*

Examining the scenes of the Gare d'Orsay with you was most pleasant. I have been there quite often at that hour and always alone. I will see your face beside me, but not with sadness, for it will be a continuation of the present, not a regret for the past...

And, a little later:

Dear friend, you were so kind to me and so trustful that I want to write to you to have a pretext for dwelling on it further. I have done scarcely anything all day but write this letter, sharpening my impressions so that they may live again the more vibrantly. I am so much a man of letters! No, that is not really it. I write so that you will know I think of you more tenderly still. You already knew, I am sure, but it is what one knows best that one most likes to hear oneself repeat. Your presence is a sweet pleasure which permeates me all the days that follow, changing their color. Perhaps you will make me rediscover a lost interest in life: if it can be done, it will come from you because you are a true friend and because I love you.

Indeed I feel most strongly the benefit of your presence; I think about it all week; it provides a fixed point around which other moments evolve, before and after. I am hard to seduce. My first impulse is to withdraw into my shell. Despite that instinct, however, I remember very well how struck I was the first time I saw you by the absence of that affectation, which makes me shudder and turns me to ice. Since then I have felt that not only were you a woman friend, but a man too...

I will call this friend Natalis; he deserves that flowering name, and I will speak of him only so:

Natalis was already a page,
Natalis was already a woman.
He remained both page and woman,

She remained both woman and page.
She may be a page to women,
She is woman enough for a page.
If I were young, were I a page,
I would love in Natalis the woman.

Put on a doublet, put on a bodice,
You will not change your soul.
You will not fool my soul.
By the form your bodice takes.

Being indeed this double creature, how could I become close
to such a presence, not only intellectually but also emotionally,
and exchanging looks more understanding than words, awaken
and test emotions which went, perhaps, as far as love?
Gourmont described these uncertain boundaries very well:

...In friendship as in love, can one ever say exactly where lie
feelings such as ours? Where they begin? Where they end, if
there is an end? They are there, we feel them, that is enough.
One should ask no more, neither interrogate nor cross them.
Let them live freely.

Or should I uproot those feelings which I had consciously cultivated before they grew deeper, for I was no longer free, even for
an affair of the mind? Already committed elsewhere, how could I
continue this new friendship, this new love?

Should I be "The creature with gauze wings" for my friend,
and everything else for the other!

May my chivalric instincts guide this unmatched tandem,
while I kept my independence like the "wild girl of Cincinnati"
(as Salomon Reinach put it) that I was!

I once waltzed into my friend's study when I'd been out riding,
dressed "en amazone"—in a riding habit. Then I went to one of
his Sundays in more conventional attire.

"I have cancelled my day," he declared. "For myself, and for
you, if you wish."

"Then what will become of your regulars from the Mercure?"

"We already see quite enough of each other in the Rue de Condé."

"And what will your friends Apollinaire and Rouveyre say?"

"They can arrange to come and see me when they want."

"But what about Edouard Champion to whom I owe our first encounter?"

"He provided the bridge between us."

...There are men whose only mission is to serve as an intermediary for others: we cross them like bridges and go on....

It was at a party at my house, a masked ball, that we next met Edouard Champion. We had enjoyed preparing for the event, Rémy and I. I had written an invitation in verse and he felt nothing would be finer than to reproduce the handwriting itself, with a little mask in one corner. I had made my friend a mask, an old Arabian smock embroidered with saffron leaves, and wrapped a turban round his head made of one of my green silk stockings. I wore the costume of a Japanese glow-worm chaser with an electric torch hidden in a wicker basket; there I had to hand a spray of little bulbs which gave a very good imitation of the light of glow-worms, their gleams visible through my hair. Thus my guests were able to recognize me even at the bottom of the garden, dimly lit by chinese lanterns hung from the trees.

Gourmont describes the evening in *Les amis d'Edouard [Edouard's Friends]:*

> I have just come from an evening-dress ball... A dress ball amongst distinguished company is no mediocre pleasure. Men show more of their true selves when wearing a disguise than in the modern uniform; their tastes are displayed simply and joyfully. It is, perhaps, in their daily lives that they wear the thickest mask and most absolute disguise. And so it should be. Put your mask of flesh back on, my dear, the others have arrived...

We presented an 18th century comedy, *Le ton de Paris,* by the Duke of Lauzun as a kind of intermezzo, preceded by Wanda

Landowska on the harpsichord.

Rémy and I were pleased to be alone together again after the party. There was a tapestry nailed to the wall inside his doorway representing the head of a clamorous viperine, no doubt symbolizing for him that which came from outside. As soon as he recognized my ring, he would tear me from the doorstep as though rescuing me from danger. Sitting opposite him, I would observe his eyes of a pure, youthful blue, the color of young flowers under glass. Like two children living in a ruin, his eyes spread an audacious gaiety all around, soon to be troubled by a shiver of anguish... I reached impetuously across the table, putting my hand on his which were dry as parchment but, at the same time, warm, a warmth which always surprised me, as much as the sight of his thick, ruddy neck bent over a library shelf. Seated sight by side, we would set off on calm sailing trips in the old navigation book he had just brought to light. Too weak in body for pleasure, too clear-sighted to be ambitious, it did him good to sail away on the arms of an Amazon.

That summer in *La France* he recorded the various stages of a three day trip we took from Paris to Normandy on *Le Druide*, a boat I had hired. We would stop each evening at a little town or village so that Gourmont could spend the night at an inn.

Every morning, before he joined me on the boat, Gourmont would write his article "Idées du jour" for *La France;* it is not surprising, therefore, that so many are on country or riverside themes. This real journey lent a new savour to his reclusive life, whose horizons had been limited to the south by the bookstalls of the Quai Voltaire and the photographs of the Gare d'Orsay, to the east by his "Café du Flore," to the north by his garret at 71 Rue des Saints-Pères and to the west by my little temple of friendship.

We sailed as far as Caudebec where the engine drank salt, got seasick and had to take a break and continue in fresh water. Stopping at Saint-Wandrille, we went to visit Maeterlinck. That great man, already going grey, seemed forever about to take flight as the ever-moving pupils of his eyes, with their two grape green flecks, darted here and there. The gothic walls of the abbey were less his natural habitat than two large modern leather armchairs which stood in the chapterhouse.

Maeterlinck had the Belgian good sense to season his use of the mystic arts to the tastes of the day. The stew sniffed like a master chef covered him in such a cloud of steam that his real character was blurred. He spoke to Gourmont about the *Latin Mystique*, and then whispered to me, "That man is an inkpot."

Maeterlinck, the mystic on a motorcycle, looking for a life to renew, would amuse himself at home by setting up a rifle on a balcony wall and shooting a fan-shaped volley across the plain, a young girl beside him to change cartridges. Was it the same girl he married in the end? My sporting sense was affronted by such a comfortable arrangement. And that is how we left him.

Georgette Leblanc, who had accompanied us as far as the boat, climbed aboard the prow, liberty veil to the wind, but the breeze was too light and the mast too small for the figurehead she was trying to resemble.

We continued on our way, which Gourmont describes as follows:

The Seine was luminously beautiful in the morning sun... How sweetly the days passed with you, my friend! And how natural it felt to live beside you, how I love looking at you, listening to you, cherishing you! Only with you can I speak freely, albeit hesitantly, of the things which give life meaning and are the foundations of my thoughts. I am so accustomed to silence and solitude that I hardly know how to speak any more, but what deep companionship there is in the presence of Natalis, even when she is silent, or dozing in the hammock! We are fortresses to each other, impregnable fortresses perhaps, but they open their doors a crack and allow the thoughts which inhabit them to fraternize a moment, join hands and play together. Though distant I feel you still, as I stretch out my arm I can touch you, be comforted that I have sensed your presence... I felt as though those three days would never end and that is how I lived them, like a little eternity. Last night I was rocked again by the gentle rolling of the boat... I watched your boat leave, my friend. At seven o'clock, Philippe the pilot sent to ask whether I was sailing too. Alas no. Though I was ready to and I stepped back on land with all the melancholy of those who stay behind.

You will not read this letter with your full attention, for you will no longer be alone, in Mantes, but know at least that though you have left me, you have not entirely gone. There is a thread running between us, bringing you my thoughts every moment of the day, unless there be interruptions which I do not like to contemplate. I know you are always at the end of that line but I know too that you are not always listening.

Perhaps never, almost never, and I speak too softly and my voice does not carry above the noise outside me. At least it does not wound your ears nor revolt your nature, which you obey so deliciously. When one loves ones destiny, one is no longer its slave.

...My friend, I hope you find the Yonne as pleasant as the Seine and that you are not delayed by the delights of Mantes, for it looks as though the weather will break and if the storms start they may well last a long time. My boat! Say that again, and think of your boating companion. Your voice lingers in my ear and from time to time I really hear it. As I leave in the morning I catch sight of the Touring Club's landing stage. For the last few days it has been occupied by a little white boat, smaller than yours. The first day, from far off I had the illusion that you had returned and felt that little quickening of the heart when we think we see the one we love. It always gives a moment's pleasure (or half a second's) and proves we do indeed have a heart...

Fresh water is still my favorite element for its tranquil flow and the reflections which hide its depths.

I abandoned *Le Druide*, which was only hired for the summer, and was happy enough rowing on the lake in the *Bois*, accompanied at times by Rémy who, never very steady on his legs, would lean on my arm as we landed. We walked on, arm in arm, and he confided to me that if I had to go to the United States, as it seemed I might, he would be happy to go with me!

He was haunted by the idea of my leaving:

It was not until I arrived home that I found the news of your absence. No more Sundays, adieu my dream. But my friend, your letter was so tender and so delicate that I forgive it that little piece of bad news. Besides, we should not be causes of constraint to each other. You will go away again and, alas, I too will leave you! How good a letter is, then, for he who is far away and for he who stays behind!... You will get my letter tomorrow morning as though you were at the Rue Jacob and, if you were alone, I would hurry to meet you in Boulogne quite easily. If I sound so reassured it is because at the mention of the word "journey" I was filled with anguish, absurd I know, but nonetheless real. Like a flash of lightning the dreaded Ohio passed over me. London, what a relief!

In *Souvenirs de mon commerce* André Rouveyre analyses in his inimitable style Rémy de Gourmont's friendship with the Amazon; thus all that is left for me to do is to put my own adventure into perspective.

Friendship is, perhaps, an imported sentiment in which most French people have little interest. Inclined toward material and abstract pleasures they have no room for this extravagance. And even a Celt like Rémy de Gourmont might never have enjoyed such a singular sentiment had he not discovered the use of his most secret aspirations.

Devastated of flesh, in revolt against God, resisting all belief systems, he at last found in friendship, that religion of intimacy, a compromise between love and religion.

As for the letters which sprang from that friendship, they were often a reply to some question raised during our conversations, which he would develop at leisure when alone. His head bursting with ideas which he had been unable to express in my presence, no matter how habitual it became, he would go and write them down and, before he sent them to the *Mercure*, I would comment as I read them with him. I would read and he would watch me reading, and that was the moment of intensity he had been waiting for. What would I say about it, what would I not say, preoccupied him so passionately that I got the following impression: pant-

ing as he stood on the lookout for my thought, he would intercept
it before it was half-formed. Thus he had the joy of seeing his
privileged reader react directly to the impression he had just
created... and of feeling that he was able to communicate with all
his readers through me.

This is how Rémy de Gourmont recalls the first of his *Lettres à
l'amazone* which I read in manuscript:

> You know that nothing passes unnoticed before my eyes
> which, though they do not see very far, see extremely well close
> up. So you will not resent my having watched you living and
> breathing while you read my first Lettre à l'amazone...
>
> ...I hope the proofs of the fifth letter will arrive tomorrow. I
> am not very happy with them. Your opinion will be very useful.
> You are the only person to whom I have ever submitted if not
> my feelings, at least my intelligence. If I dared I would have you
> read everything I write...
>
> ...Precious friend, I have taken the greatest advantage of your
> clear thinking. I have worked on this bungled letter for most of
> the morning, cut out many words and added some phrases. So
> it will be less unworthy of you...

The feelings which developed between us, from 1910 until his
death in 1915, make clear to me his touching constancy with
regard to me, if not mine toward him. He wrote to me:

> I no longer expected or wanted anything from life. You came
> and resuscitated me. I live, I loved you, I love you. I owe you
> that, I owe you everything, sweet friend.

Despite the most absorbing of passions, I do not believe I ever
failed our friendship which continues to obsess me, as he himself
recognized in the last letter he sent:

> Yesterday, my friend, I was made more than ever aware of
> your goodness and tenderness. You wanted to console me
> and in place of my sadness you aroused deep joy. How many
> times have I repressed the impulse which propels me toward

you in an unconquerable emotion! Yesterday my heart leapt out despite me and I could not resist. What a moment! I nearly fainted and, divinely wounded, I remained for a long time in a state of agitation. The strange, injurious power I have over myself suddenly abandoned me when I saw the blue eyes I so love dilate and your eyelids redden... My friend, I can scarcely think, scarce write, I would like you to read my heart, and you can read it, can you not?... I begin to recover myself again in my weakened mind. I have never been so happy, have perhaps never suffered so much from being a feeble invalid for so long and will perhaps never fully recover my strength. I need you to comfort me for that too.

Here are some flowers...

Here are some fruit...

I cannot say that. I feel as though I come to you with empty hands! What pain in the midst of joy! But there is something I can offer you, sweet friend, the love which grows each day in my heart.   —Rémy

During the summer of 1914 I was summoned to return home. My luggage had already been packed up and shipped out from Le Havre on one of the last transatlantic liners, but I could not make up my mind to follow, leave France during such an ordeal, and tear myself away from the love that was indispensable to me and from the friendship which counted on my presence.

Detained in Normandy during the autumn of 1915, I did not see Rémy critically ill, nor dying, nor on his death bed.

I did not go to his funeral, I hardly know where his grave is.

Each of us is devout in their own fashion, each of us lives with our dead and keeps them alive in ourselves.

Ceaselessly contemplating an end is a way of creating it. I did not go and gaze upon his absence through the half open door. I did not walk through the ante-room, past his book-shelves to the largest room where his table spread out beneath a latticed window. I did not muse over his reed pen, the dried ink in the hidden ink well, the letter format paper awaiting his tiny handwriting, each word neatly separated, its silhouette clearly outlined on the evenly-spaced lines and, between the lines, here and there a burn from a cigarette spark, a punctuation mark showing that his attention had been seized by some unattainable thought, or simply the rolling of another pinch of tobacco which, too thick for the skimpy paper, flared and fell.

I did not see him show me out, one last time, and stand on the landing, watching me go down the stairs. He could see no more than my hand on the bannisters, polished by much use, or my smile floating up to him through the gas lights on the spiral staircase, interminable as that of a tower. The walls slid smoothly between the floors, with no other roughness than the Gas Company boxes. When I reached the courtyard (where a rabbit grazed peacefully round the lone tree), I would give a last glance upward. He was there. Moved at feeling so discreetly observed, I would go out. I never saw his door close behind him...

Gertrude Stein*

This is a tentative approach to Gertrude Stein and to a variety of her writings as yet unpublished.

The title of this fourth volume is to be *As fine as Melanchtha*, which, itself is an appreciation that cannot be surpassed.

How did this title come about?

An editor asked Miss Stein to write something as fine as her story *Melanchtha* from *Three Lives*; and so she did. Did she?

I have not yet received the manuscript of the book I have been asked to preface, and because a book may not need a preface but a preface certainly needs a book, I have in the meantime been given *carte blanche* to write whatever I like. Therefore, leaving the future readers to their diverse impressions, I prefer to relate my personal experience and points of contact and discord with this author, whose companionship I delighted in and now cherish.

In recalling so magnetic a personality, how not, first of all, evoke this magnet to which so many adhered? For she attracted and influenced not only writers, but painters, musicians, and least but not last, disciples. She used to declare "I don't mind meeting anyone once," but she rarely kept to so strict a limitation. Although the most affirmative person I ever met, she was a keen and responsive listener.

"Life is as others spoil it for us," concluded a beautiful friend of mine who had become a derelict through her fatalism. How many spoilt lives came to Gertrude with their misfortunes, due to some inexplicable situation or sentimental rut? She, instead of offering helpless sympathy, often helped them out, by changing an *idée fixe* or obsession into a fresh start in a new direction.

As an appreciative pupil of William James, her study in reac-

tions also proved salutary to the *spoilers* of lives. In these she sometimes detected a genius for deceit which she would aid them to
confess, or she would indicate means to liberate them of their victims, since as Henry James—was it not?—wisely remarked,
"There is only one thing worse than a tyrant and that is a tyrant's
victim."

Even more interested in cases than in their curse, many served
as characters in one of her plays and stories. Some of them may
even discover themselves in this very book... that is, if they are sufficiently initiated into Miss Stein's game of blind man's buff, or
blind man's bluff, in which the reader is blind-folded—obscurity
being the better part of discretion as to who is who. At other times
she issued works of a most penetrating and acute quality, filled
with subtle analysis, like *Things as they are.*

Even I, who am not in the habit of consulting anybody about
my dilemmas, once brought a problem of mine to the willing and
experienced ear of Gertrude. In a moment, in a word, she diag-
nosed the complaint: "*Consanguinity.*"

She never appeared to hesitate or reflect or take aim, but invariably hit the mark.

Our Walks

Often in the evening we would walk together; greeted at the
door of 5 rue Christine by Gertrude's staunch presence, the pleasant touch of hand, the well-rounded voice always ready to
chuckle. Our talks and walks led us far from war paths. For generally having no axe to grind nor anyone to execute it with, we felt
detached and free to wander in our quiet old quarter where, while
exercising her poodle, "Basket", we naturally fell into thought and
step. Basket, unleashed, ran ahead, a white blur, the ghost of a dog
in the moonlight side-streets:

Where ghost and shadows mingle—
As lovers, lost when single.

The night's enchantment made our conversation as light, iri-
descent and bouncing as soap bubbles, but as easily exploded
when touched upon—so I'll touch on none of them for you, that

a bubble may remain a bubble! And perhaps we never said "d'impérissable choses." *

We also met during Gertrude Stein's lionized winter of 1934-35 in New York, and walked into one of its flashing, diamond sharp days, where what one touches brings sparks to the finger tips.

Witnessing with apprehension Gertrude's independent crossing of streets without a qualm, I asked her why she never wavered on the edge of curb-stones, as I did with one foot forward and one foot backward, waiting for a propitious crowd and signal.

"All these people, including the nice taxi-drivers, recognize and are careful of me." So saying, she set forth, her longish skirt flapping sail-like in a sea-breeze, and landed across 59th Street in the Park, as confidently as the Israelistes over the isthmus of the Red Sea—while we, not daring to follow in her wake, risked being engulfed.

She accepted her fame as a tribute, long on the way but due, and enjoyed it thoroughly. Only once, in Paris—and indeed the last time I saw her—did the recognition of a cameraman displease her, for he waylaid her just as we were entering Rumpelmeyer's pâtisserie. In order to satisfy her need for the cake, and the photographer's wish, she was photographed by him, through the plate-glass window, eating the chosen one. Her eagerness was partly caused by a disappointing lunch we had just experienced at Prunier's, where each sort of sea-food we ordered—prompted by appetites accrued by our recent war-time privations, and still existing restrictions,—was denied us, until at last (this was in 1946), driven to despair of a better world, Gertrude dropped her head between her hands and shook it from side to side; and not until we reached that rue de Rivoli pâtisserie did her spirits and appetite revive and meet with partial compensation.

Their Cakes

The discovery of cakes had always been a peace-time pursuit of Gertrude and Alice. Meeting them by chance at Aix-les-Bains, I enquired what happened to be on this opposite bank of the Lac

---

*Baudelaire

du Bourget, and was informed of a new sort of cake created in one of the villages on a mountain beyond. But first obliged to go on other errands, they descended from the lofty seat of their old Ford car, Alice bewildered as an idol and Gertrude with the air of an Indian divinity. As they disappeared around a corner, not without causing wonderment, the only appropriate offering seemed to me one of those long, house-stemmed lotus flowers of dark pink, which I purchased and stuck between the spokes of Gertrude's steering wheel—with a card of explanation: "A wand to lead you on."

Another meeting with this inseparable couple took place in their *jardin de cure* at Bilignin, on another summer afternoon. It somewhat resembled the book-cover Cecil Beaton designed for Gertrude Stein's *Wars I have Seen*, only a huge parasol replaced the parachutes and we sat peacefully on gayly striped canvas chairs. The four of us—for Romaine Brooks had come along with me,—and Basket, all curves and capers, lent a circus effect to the scene. As China tea was being served, Alice placed on the round outdoor table a fluffy confection of hers—probably a coconut layer cake which only Americans know how to make—and eat. Its white icing, edged with ornamental pink, matched Basket's like coating and incidental pinks. Gertrude sat in the favorite position in which Picasso portrayed her, clothed in rough attire with moccasined feet, knees apart, reminiscent of the gypsy queen under her tent in my old Bar Harbor days.

Meanwhile Romaine Brooks contemplated our group and finding it "paintable", wished to start a picture of it then and there, before the light of her inspiration should fade. But, I the disturbing element of the party, because of a clock in my mind and in duty bound to pleasures, insisted that Romaine and I were due elsewhere. So this picture of us all was left unpainted: *mea culpa!*

Gertrude's and Alice's flair for cakes makes me conclude that while poets are left to starve in garrets—or, as here in France, in *chambres de bonnes*, living only in the past and future, with the hope of an aftermath of fame, an author such as Gertrude Stein, admitting of nothing but a "continuous present", must be sustained on sweetmeats and timely success—this being the surest way of taking the cake and of eating and having it too.

Faith In Herself

Her belief in herself never failed her. Even when still a child, she and her brother Leo used to discuss who would prove to be their family's genius. Leo thought himself that predestined genius; but Gertrude, turning to us—her two visitors were that afternoon Madame de Clermont-Tonnerre and myself—emphatically declared: "But, as you know, it turned out to be me!"

Indeed, such a faith in oneself "passeth understanding," and what a poor thing is understanding, compared to such a faith!

As faith is far more exulting than reason, she once deplored Ezra Pound's becoming "the village explainer," which led so great a poet, and discoverer of poets, to his present standstill.

Her Lecture At Oxford

From the crest of Gertrude Stein's tidal wave of success, she was persuaded by Harold Acton to lecture a class of students at Oxford University, and she managed to hold them spellbound without a single concession to meet their understanding. Her lecture soared above theirs as they sensed something that surpassed them, but which neither freed their laughter nor their judgement, so that nothing was left to them but to uproariously applaud.

She afterwards consented to meet them on their level, and both their questions and her answers were reported: inspiring and inspired.

With Our G.I.'s

The same democratic spirit made her popular with our G.I.'s of the second world war. They also gathered something unique from her presence amongst them, and so she led them, as a sort of *vivandière de l'esprit*, from war into peace, and to realize their own, instead of their collective, existence. But in some cases this change was hard to bring about, loathe as they were to be "separated from," no longer "club together, be part of, belong to," etc. This fact was brought to even my notice in Florence by a big G.I. who confessed to me that "the urge to join his comrades was so strong that he couldn't even stop a moment to brush his teeth!" The disbanding of the herd instinct—to re-become individual and perhaps a nobody instead of leaving it to a chief in command with everything settled for you (death included), to take off a uniform to become uniform—all of this was more than some of them could stand.

And how not feel homesick for their regiment when forced homeward, perhaps to intrude on a family, or face hostile businessmen? At such a moment a Gertrude Stein met them with her invigorating affirmations and cheered them up.

It must have been about this period that she was photographed against our Stars and Stripes.

Becoming Singular

Patriotic as Gertrude Stein seemed, she certainly dispelled our discouraging axiom that "one man's as good as another". No one has dared to say this of the American woman!

From her *Making of Americans*, I translated into French some of her most significant pages on our "progress in becoming singular". These pages were read—between the wars—in my salon, at meetings destined to bring about a better *entente* between French, English and American authors.

On my "Friday" celebrating Gertrude Stein, Mina Loy addressed them by explaining her admiration for this innovator who "swept the literary circus clear for future performances."

Many examples, including her own, were read to this effect—and a zeal for translating seized upon many of us from then on.

We doubt if she ever thought of her readers at all.

In going over my impressions of her—*de vive voix, de vive mémoire*—in these fragmentary evidences, I find that I have somewhat replaced the essential by the superficial. I suppose that to want to enjoy and know such a personage without going into their more original ambitions and works is like seizing chance reflections from a water-mirror regardless of its depth; this is what I find myself doing here, and avoiding the significance of her under-sea mysteries. Yet I have tried to dive deeper, and only touched rock-bottom to be ejected up again to the surface, suffocating with too much salt water, in search of too rare a pearl.

Being a writer of *pensées,* I like to find a thought as in a nut or sea-shell, and while I make for a point, Gertrude seems to proceed by avoiding it. And this I am told, in order to create an atmosphere, "a picture," not through connections but disconnections. And her rotative system consists in getting at a subject by going not for but around it, in snowball fashion, gathering up everything she meets on her rounds.

She also has a marked preference for "similarity" as opposed to "contrast"—a method which has long proved effective in rituals and incantations. As for her repetitions, they seem to me just a way of making time before finding out what to say next, and remind me of those long sermons bringing about a retarded comprehension to audiences under the mixed fumes of incense and music. But I also remember how glad we were, as children, on the "merry-go-round," of a second and third chance to catch onto the golden ring.

And did not the child-woman, Mélisande, by saying "*Je ne suis pas heureuse*" (which is human) gain an echo's magic by repeating it—aided by Debussy's accompaniment?

Her System of "Hide And Go Seek"

Is not Gertrude Stein's example most stimulating, until she goes too far in the practice of it? Systems are apt to run away with their inventors, or else someone else catches on to them and uses them to a better effect. While, as in this instance, the inventor remains either monotonous or bewildering. Here Gertrude warns us that "Bewildering is a word that carried no weight". But what of monotonous? And why must she, who can be so startlingly inventive, risk misleading us through such a wilderness of words?

If her meaning were only obscured by density, as in Joyce's *Work in Progress* or Ezra Pound's *Cantos,* I could be all for it—as for other breakers of routine, such as Remy de Gourmont's "dissociation of ideas;" but I cannot see where so simple a dissociation of words from their subject leads us.

However I suppose that there comes a transition period in civilization, where words as well as ideas need to be divorced in order to regain new vitality and freer associations.

And indeed one must not be too bent on understanding or one misses essential results. So I must either play this writer's "hide and seek," or stand by my preference for her more comprehensible publications.

Still envying her knights errant: Thornton Wilder, Scott Fitzgerald, Hemingway, Carl Van Vechten, Bernard Fay, Max White etc., for being initiated and able to spin, undazed, around her circles, closing us out from:

> Thoughts hardly to be packed
> Into a narrow act,
> Fancies that broke through language and escaped.
> (Robert Browning: *Rabbi Ben Ezra*)

Yet why must her fancies prove so discouraging? But we must be patient with artists, as they are most patient with themselves, and follow themselves even where we cannot follow them.

Struggling Towards A Conclusion

> My idle hands are stained with ink,
> And still I don't know what I think!

And this remains my state of mind even now, when the manuscript shipped across the ocean for my introduction has at last arrived.

Must I confess, at once, much to the amusement of Paul Valéry, "J'ai peur de lire"—and should I not all the more fear to read, lest my commenting results in betrayal either so near a neighbor or myself?

How shrink such a responsibility—which Carl Van Vechten and Donald Gallup so imprudently entrusted to me? By arguing that a long preface would misrepresent a book of short stories—and especially of these stories without a story! Besides agreeing with whomever first apologized for writing at too great a length—not having taken pains to make it short. I have always had a predilection for what is short, and especially novels and long stories often seem to me much longer than life, and far less interesting.

Up Against Volume IV

But here is that big white block of a manuscript awaiting my hazardous inscriptions—as though this fourth cornerstone of Gertrude Stein's unpublished works were not better without. Even so must I, after so much hesitation vainly expressed to the sponsors of these posthumous works, pursue? And now, as I start turning over this typewritten manuscript, Gertrude sympathetically comes out to meet me with such consoling phrases as:

> Nobody knows what I'm trying to do, but I do, and I know when I succeed.
> What can be expected of paragraphs and sentences by the time I'm done.
> That is a sentence but two words cannot make a preface.
> It was exasperating, we were patient, we said it again and meant everything.
> I have often remarked that invention—and there is a great deal of invention—I have often remarked that invention concerns itself with inventing, and I, I feel no responsibility.

Are not such phrases self-explanatory? But it is hard not to resent a method which allows its author to write so many dull pages on purpose. And then again one is suddenly awakened to remarkable remarks, such as:

> A sentence speaks loudly.
> A noun is nature personified.
> How many Saints are irreligious?
> I feel the value of religions—all religions.

And such glimpses into her unwritten novels:

> Always she knew she would be everything—he always knew he was becoming.
> She is his second life.
> How can you be so radiantly far?…
> Hurry to me restfully.

Eclipsing my feeling.
I did not think I ever could be cross again with love.
How dearly is she me, how dearly is she me, how
dearly how very dearly am I she."

And what a fresh beauty in such definitions as:

Civilization begins with a rose.
This is the flower of my leaf."

And what she must have had with:

I have invented many titles and sub-titles:
Please prepare the bed for Mrs. Henry. Dear dear this is a
title!

My Attempts At Imitation
I wondered if I could make up Steinean sentences, and succeed
in breaking sense away from sense. It's hard to get something to
mean nothing and nothing to mean something. I have tried and
this is the result:

Did I like it? Did I like liking it? Or I dislike liking it or did I
dislike it or dislike disliking it? Or did I dislike liking to dislike it?
Or did I like disliking to like it?

You see it is harder than one thinks not to make sense. And we
are never sure of being foolproof. For example:

Did Tom fool? Did Tomfoolery fool? Did fool foolery fool
Tom?

I have written a whole page full of this sort of things, but feel it
would be inappropriate to quote more of it here. For, enough is
already more than enough of this sort of juggling with words.

"Enter These Enchanted Woods"
I have examined many of the leaves of this forest of words and
lost myself in their midst, missing not only my way but hers. Perhaps there are signs and paths through it which I fail to sense, so I

prefer to stay on its border and hunt for the wild flowers amongst the leaves. Leaving the author's knights errant to penetrate her mysteries. The spirit of them invites trespassers more adventurous than I have proved.

"Enter these enchanted woods, ye who dare."

(George Meredith)

Alice B. Toklas having intimated to me, in her mild but persuasive way, to cease beating around the bush and picking up only the chance plums that fall from it, I have read steadily through *Did Nellie and Lilly love you.* Though I can't make out whether they did or didn't—the chances being two against one they didn't.

I like this kind of novel, but that's perhaps because I don't like novels. This chapter contains none of the usual or unusual subjects, intrigues, or relations and sequences, not a climax to a more or less fictitious end. Certain words acting as highlights lead the way, but to no conclusions, or to conclusions left to the reader and interchangeable enough to suit more cases than one, more love affairs than one, and to more marriages giving no clue. If clue there be, it is left to our discretion: the clue is perhaps you. Our approach remains that of the eavesdropper on situations to which we have not been initiated. At least this discretion spares us the embarrassing complexity through which we have too often witnessed the love-scenes in book, play, and film—especially in those moving-pictures where the sexually-starved feed their emotions on the hero and heroine's uniting in that culminating inevitable and prolonged kiss (a kiss which should, in natural sequence, precipitate the couple off to bed).

The subjects of this book are divertingly different: in *A Third* it must be very interesting for the three concerned, that is if no one of the three remains the third.

Equally so. *A Description of all the Incidents which I have Observed in Travelling and on my Return,* leaves open the question "Whether one receives more letters at home or abroad?"—One of the determining questions as to whether to travel or not to travel.

The portrait of *Miss Cruttwell* was taken from the life of a real person, but she is treated so that no one would recognize her—not even Miss Cruttwell herself!

In *No*—if "Yes is for a very young man," *No* should be for a very old man and wise one.

The Background of a Detective Story—if the best detective story is the one whose mystery remains complete and the crime undiscovered, this one would win!

In *One Sentence*, how well its author has imitated the cacklings of an "elderly couple talking much much or much talking too much too much!"

And "She means nothing wrong but the love of talking is so strong in her that I think it necessary to check it whenever I can."

"A little example does make it thin it makes it very colored very colored white."

What *One Sentence* says has as much relation to speech as when a parrot first tries to vocalize part of a conversation just overheard!

It is obvious that in *A history of having a great many times not continued to be friends*, her friendships ceased from the causes already detected in their beginning.

Other pieces are so much less comprehensible that I can make neither head nor tail of them, but nevertheless feel something like the first principles of life interestingly astir in their middle.

Then again I find many treasures in this version of *As fine as Melanchtha*—as though she, Melanchtha, had fled from giving herself a rival self, but not without leaving behind for us her jewel-case, containing such gems as—but these, as the rest, I must now leave Gertrude's readers to discover. With my apology for detaining them—if I have detained them—so long.

17th January, 1954

When Poets Meet

Hazardous as it may seem to try and bring about a meeting between poets, the 'animatrice' of Shakespeare and Company in Paris attempted such a feat. In the lull between wars, when the turtle dove was again to be heard in the land, Sylvia Beach gathered us together in her bookshop at 12 Rue de l'Odéon for an evening lecture, where we were to listen to what Edith Sitwell had to say about Gertrude Stein—and in Miss Stein's expectant presence.

These two interesting women had already met, down in their intervening valley, and become friendly, and had even exchanged messages to one another from their respective hill-tops. But this reunion was to be more than a brief 'exposé' of mutual understanding and admiration—more like a sort of pact for probing, 'séance tenante,' the mysterious vaults of another's mind, and that might bring to light yet unminted treasures. Much as a fellow-miner invited to prospect the property of his neighbor might hit upon a lucky vein to exploit. So at the appointed hour of 9 p.m. we waited in confident silence that some such miracle should be performed before us, and Miss Stein's much-disputed effigy cleared and coined into never-to-be-forgotten words.

Edith Sitwell sat well and majestically remote above her audience. Her long Elizabethan hands, bearing no papers, met in their virginal loveliness, sufficient unto themselves. Her voice also had a rare quality of detachment, as it rose on the capricious wings of thought to nameless heights. And we wondered if this singular prelude was meant to prepare us for even rarer revelations. Although the actual name of Gertrude Stein was not yet mentioned we felt nevertheless initiated, even by so round-about an approach, which would surely soon emerge into a striking view of the rival summit. But no such view appeared, as Edith Sitwell, seemingly forgetful of its co-existence, opened a book, amongst those on the table before her, and rose to read.

Ah yes, of course, we were first to be given a chosen page of Gertrude Stein's writing. But what were those strange sounding, un-Steinian rhythms now scanned by this unique poetess's lips? Were they not some of Miss Sitwell's very own? So she proceeded, resembling Mallarmé's "Hérodiade": "*Oui, c'est pour moi que je fleuris déserte*"—for was she not also caught in the magic circle of self—and apparently quite oblivious of the object of our reunion. However, did we not detect a faint gleam of suppressed mirth filtering down to us through her blond eyelashes, as she turned the page to read on? Here again we were forced to recognize a strongly accentuated melody, somehow dedicated, rather than to Miss Stein, to the Negro race.

We dared not communicate a smile of surprise; and indeed Gertrude Stein's expression was forbidding. For this was not fair play to her, nor destined to cover the ground agreed upon. Yet she sat bolt upright, meditating, in spite of a twitch of her hands, a more gentlemanly reprisal than immediate exposure. And she preserved this ominous attitude throughout the rest of the lecture. Although it would have seemed a relief if, then and there, she had cleared the atmosphere by an almighty exit. But no—she remained on, intent, and we all listened to this singular monologue devoted exclusively to Miss Sitwell's self. And when it was ended, boastfully or faintly applauding, we forthwith united in an intimate *petit souper* in Sylvia Beach's apartment upstairs—where I proceeded to offer "orangeade" or "sherry" while our hostess, aided by her neighbor, Adrienne Monnier, from the precious bookshop opposite, passed sandwiches and cakes.

The glass of sherry I proferred Edith Sitwell made her question: "Won't it go to my head?" I smilingly reassured her and refrained from murmuring, "No spirits but Miss Sitwell's own could accomplish that!" For our tacit *consigne* had simultaneously been to act as though nothing unusual had happened—nor indeed had it!

Turning around to serve Gertrude Stein, I perceived with awe that she had gone home. So no "toasts" followed, nor indeed were any *de circonstance*, lest they come from embittered cups! Yet on retiring, I promised myself that should I ever again face Miss Sitwell, I would recall this lecture and ask her why she had allowed it to so miscarry. To which she would doubtless, and perhaps even with a maidenly blush, charmingly answer: "Ah yes, I did mean to speak about dear Gertrude Stein, but became otherwise inspired."

Part Six: Natalie and Anti-Semitism

An Afterword by Anna Livia

The Trouble with Heroines:
Natalie Clifford Barney and Anti-Semitism

The trouble with heroines is that as soon as we discover their
feet of clay, they become the scapegoat of our common failings as
surely as, in their pre-lapsarian state, they embodied our common
ideals. That Natalie Clifford Barney has been a kind of heroine
there can be little doubt. Hailed by Bertha Harris [Vida 1978:
257] as the first known lesbian since Sappho (twenty-four centu-
ries down the line), her retreat to Lesbos with Renée Vivien to
recreate a Sapphic poetry community, her literary salon in Paris,
her outspoken declaration of "the perilous advantage" of "being
other than normal" [Barney 1960: 23], the long and exuberant list
of her love affairs—the last of which began on a park bench in
1954 when she was seventy-eight years old—have made her something of a latter day lesbian star.

As she wrote almost entirely in French and had not, until
today, been translated she was known to anglophones by her
deeds rather than her words. So I began the weighty task of reading through her collected works, the various biographies and the
special editions of magazines dedicated to her, in order to produce
the collection you now hold in your hands. I would be asked at
dinner parties what I was working on and, replying, "Natalie Clifford Barney," I expected the usual post Jean Chalon response,
"What? The lesbian Don Juan?" generated by his biography, *Portrait of a Seductress.* Instead my hosts said, "You? I wouldn't have
thought... I mean, wasn't she... She was a fascist, an anti-semite,
didn't I read that somewhere?" They probably did read that somewhere, for feminist scholars, Karla Jay and Shari Benstock, have
both commented on this unsavory side of Barney's life in their
respective texts, *The Amazon and the Page* and *Women of the Left*

Bank. Someone referred me to pages 412-418 of Benstock's book which quote the following paragraph from Barney's *Memoirs of a European American,* her unpublished war notebooks of 1940-44:

> The trade of usury has proved the most lucrative and far reaching: practised openly in well-defined quarters, it was long tolerated and even found useful. But since these usurers have dissimulated themselves, that they might more easily mix with and "fix" the Gentiles, they very much resent having their maneuvers divulged, as recently distinguished by the obligatory wearing of a yellow star. Yet other nations and trades are proud of their insignia. Should they not rather imitate that German Jewess who had her star made up of yellow diamonds and wore it as proudly as a German his swastika? (144-145)

Since it seemed the bulk of the evidence pointing to Barney's anti-semitism came from her unpublished memoirs, I felt a moral obligation to go and read the manuscript for myself before completing *A Perilous Advantage* and presenting "the best of Natalie Clifford Barney".

But, was it fair to judge Barney on one unpublished manuscript which, had it not been for modern researchers, might never have seen the light of day? Are there also signs of anti-semitism in Barney's published works? Sadly, yes, there are. It can be seen in a scattering of aphorisms:

> What nation will love the Jews so well that they may stop being Jewish? [Barney 1910: 66]

> Those dispossessed Jews who seem to have accepted their burden of guilt and their inheritance, the crown of thorns, still pale to think of a god's agony—but perhaps all crowns are crowns of thorns! [Barney 1918: 27]

> A straightened Jewish nose: surgery, paraffin or mixed ancestry? [Barney 1918; 129]

These are the usual slings and arrows of anti-semitism: blaming the Jews for the death of Christ, mocking Semitic physical features, suggesting that if only Jews would assimilate they would no longer have a problem. (I say 'they' since I am not Jewish but an Anglo-Irish Protestant—ethnically speaking). Other aphorisms suggest a more ambiguous, even contradictory attitude. Among the series of dedications which open the *Pensées d'une amazone* one finds:

To those who force me to remain Israfel [Barney 1918:VI]
(A play on words indicating an intemingling of Israel and the Angel Raphael: Barney's cultural heritage.)
More than the American, the Jew talks through his nose: but also with his eyes and spirit. [Barney 1918: 129]

Usually when Barney speaks of 'the Jews' she speaks from a distance, producing nicely worded social witticisms to please her salon public. Yet her mother's father, Samuel Pike, was Jewish. Barney recalls that the Lithuanian poet, Milosz, used to say that one needed to be part Jewish, as both he and she were, in order to understand the world. Barney evidently agreed. Later, at dinner at her house Milosz exploded into vicious, rather unexpected invective against "the chosen cursed people, that race unworthy of its kings and prophets who failed in their sacred mission and became merchants, thrown out of the temple in times gone by." [Barney 1960: 214-215]. Samuel Pike had been a merchant and had devoted a large part of his wealth to building the first opera house the good citizens of Cincinnati had ever known. When it burned down, uninsured, he built another one.

Was Barney aware of the contradictions of her position? It's unclear. In one of her collections of literary portraits, *Souvenirs indiscrets*, she repeats a tale told her by Elisabeth de Gramont, Duchess de Clermont-Tonnerre, allegedly one of her lovers:

During the occupation, obliged to come in person to get her ration card and seeing two queues in front of her, she went and stood at the end of the shortest. Then, holding her lorgnette to her eye, she noticed that the people in front of her were wearing the gold star. She slipped over to the other queue—but not without attracting the attention of the German officer who, suspecting some illegality, demanded: "Since when have you had the right to stand on this side?"

"Since Henry the Fourth," she replied. [Barney 1960:130-131]

An amusing anecdote of the triumph of the French aristocracy over grubby German bureaucrats. But what about the people in the other queue? How long did they wait? Were their ration cards different from the others'? Did they get the same food ration? What happened to those people? We are not told: these questions are irrelevant compared to the demands of salon wit. With a similar flippancy Barney relates, in her unpublished memoir, a funny story someone had told her of a woman in occupied Paris who received a phone call from someone asking, "Is this Mrs. Levy?" To which the woman replied, "No, Madame, certainly not, I have quite enough worries as it is." [Barney MS: 185]

But the portrait of Elisabeth de Gramont continues, and the situation becomes more complex. In 1934 she had received the Légion d'Honneur, yet ten years later her title, her honors, her talent got her nowhere; she even found it hard to get paid for her work (she was a writer and historian). Barney comments:

Perhaps people thought she was rich because of her half-brothers and half-sister whose mother was a Rothschild.
[Barney 1960: 131-132]

So Gramont's siblings were Jewish. Had this endangered her life during the war? Barney does not say, though friends of hers were interned and deported: Barney comments in her memoirs that Colette's husband, Maurice Goudeket, was interned, released and spent the rest of the war in hiding.

Despite the experience of her friends, Barney writes slightingly, even appreciatively of 'the wars of extermination.' In two separate passages where she abhors the way men condemn women to the agony of childbirth and exults in the fact that homosexuals do, at least, not breed, which have strong feminist and homophile overtones, she writes:

Since nature invented a horrific and almost unavoidable method of giving birth and surviving, doubtless civilization wanted to lend a hand by offering its apparatus for extermination. [Barney 1918: 18]

Since neither wars of extermination nor birth control have been sufficient to limit the population, why does it not occur to the Lord of Lords to change his slogan to "Stay home and stop multiplying?" [Barney 1963: 166]

More witty Barneyisms, typically ignoring the full import of those "wars of extermination." Did she ignore it, or was she ignorant?

Barney expressed strong support for feminism; she recounts how she and her sister became feminists as children, when they saw a woman and a dog pulling a milk cart while the man strolled alongside smoking his pipe. Yet one comes across aphorisms of hers which are profoundly misogynist:

Sentimentality is lady's work.
Rape is perhaps not the least desirable way of pleasing.
[Barney 1918: 94]

The flighty female:
The child who has been raped walks away sucking happily on a stick of barley sugar. [Ibid.]

These seem randomly unpleasant, infrequent echoes of the jokes men of her class might make about women, oddly out of keeping with Barney's life and attitudes. Can one put her anti-semitic 'sallies' into the same box labelled "random unpleasantness due to class position and prevailing social attitudes"? Had Barney grown more conservative with age, or rather, more conservative with *the* age, for 1930s Europe was a far cry from the Naughty Nineties and the Belle Epoque? Was she incapable of understanding social formations more complex than those involving a tête-à-tête? Had she fallen into bad company?—the splenetic separatist Renée Vivien replaced by a morose misanthropic Romaine Brooks, passionate admirer of Gabriele D'Annunzio, the Italian poet who gave Mussolini the title 'Il Duce'; their good friend Ezra

Pound, making his passionate pro-fascist radio broadcasts throughout the war, passionately listened to by Romaine and Natalie. For Natalie always sided with passion.

I went to Paris to try and answer these questions and read my way through the *Memoirs of a European American*, all three hundred and something pages of it. I studied other unpublished manuscripts and private notebooks. The Memoirs are a mixture of war commentary, political theory and daily life in fascist Italy, from Mussolini through the arrival of first German, then British and finally American troops, interspersed with reminiscences, and speeches by Hitler and Mussolini.

Exactly what Barney chose to quote is telling. Until three quarters of the way through she strongly disagreed with the Allies, seeing them as war loving destroyers of life and, more importantly, art. This was, no doubt, the local Italian version of events and it would be hard to blame Barney for believing it without at the same time condemning recent American support for the destruction of Iraq. Many Americans, reading only U.S. coverage of the Gulf War, knew little of the suffering of the Iraqis and the terrible devastation of their country. It is surely a truism that war reporting is biased in favor of the "home team." Barney makes continual reference to Hitler and Mussolini's offer of peace, copying out Hitler's *Last Appeal to Reason* [Barney MS: 53] and his Munich speech of 8th November 1940, concluding that Hitler's outstretched hand had been refused whereupon he had gracefully turned the gesture into a fascist salute [Barney MS: 13]. Barney takes seriously the German suggestion that the French send their unemployed workers to Germany to relieve French POWs, and criticises the French government for refusing [Barney MS: 150]. She blames the English for bombing open towns and sinking unarmed ships, meanwhile praising Mussolini for gathering together the free spirits of Italy and binding them together into a "fascio."

Many of Barney's comments on the events of the war are such ridiculous trivialisations that one must seriously ask how much she understood. She suggests that "our boys," (the American GIs), be served mint tea in place of alcohol [Barney MS: 157], is charmed that the Italian soldiers are as keen on *gelati* as the GIs are on beer, and listens with amusement as the military band drops into popular operatic arias once their drill is over [p. 208]. She complains, after the bombing has begun, that her new maid entered her service "merely for the purpose of eating." She recalls how her French chauffeur was seized while cherry-picking and taken to what she terms a "concentration camp," a nice little mountain chalet where four gentlemen were being kept. After doing the housework (which he enjoys), the chauffeur is free to bathe under a waterfall and spend his tips in the village [p. 33].

At many points in the manuscript she states that she is not, and never has been, interested in politics.

> Whatever my passions had been they were no-wise political. [p. 179]

If this is so, why copy out Hitler's speeches? As she notes earlier:

> Possessed of few convictions, I felt an urgent need to pick some up. [p. 72-73]

If you seek refuge in a fascist country, the easiest ideas to pick up will undoubtedly be fascist. Toward the end of the war, after the Allied victory in Italy, Barney and Brooks learn they are to be interviewed about their war loyalties. Barney expects an upper-class Englishman and is completely at a loss when a scruffy young Italian turns up. She leaves all the talking to Romaine, saying that the man is clearly incapable of understanding anything. Romaine told him that they were "artists, who knew too little about politics to take any part in them." [p. 295].

In her apparent determination to remain frivolous in the face of war, ("To be wounded or killed on the way to or from a cup of tea would be too ridiculous" [Barney MS: 252]) Barney resembled many of her contemporaries. Gertrude Stein remarked that the Germans at Aix-les-Bains were really very nice [p.43]; Paul Poiret, the theatrical director, declared:

> I've invented an ambulance uniform with interior padding

and pockets, and a helmet-like gas-mask that will ennoble the wearer's appearance instead of making it like an animal with a snout. Everything should be beautifully thought out—whether to go to a ball or to death. [p. 41]

Although during the war years Barney's loyalties were with Hitler and Mussolini, what she was loyal to was a confused sense that tradition, artistic expression and personal freedom must prevail over the communist threat. By the end of the Memoirs, what's more, she is proudly and enthusiastically pro-American, offering free Vermouth to wandering GIs. To understand this turnabout it must be remembered that Barney was a pacifist. Though Benstock and Jay see her fascist sympathies as contradicting this, I found no evidence of a change of heart. If the events of the war are considered from the, admittedly idiosyncratic, perspective of an upper-class villa in Northern Italy, it is not hard to understand how Barney came to the conclusion that the Allies were the aggressors and the Axe, defenders of freedom; Germany was, after all, not bombing them. She demands angrily why English women didn't use their newly won vote to stop the war [p. 66], and suggests cynically that the vote was only granted to Italian and French women so that they could be forced to share the blame for the war [p. 311]. Upon hearing of the looting of Sicilian art treasures, by what she terms "Judaeo Anglo American connoisseurs," she wrote a scathingly critical letter addressed, "Dear Barbarians" [p. 194].

Barney's change of perspective on the war is brought about suddenly, can in fact be pinpointed to one hour and the spectacular events of that hour. The villa in which she and Romaine Brooks lived was requisitioned by German officers during a period of heavy bombardment. The two women, before retreating to a neighbor's cellar for the night, "soothe their highstrung nerves" listening to Peri, the neighbors' daughter, play the piano. They find the Germans "pitifully exemplary" and the following night the officers are also invited to listen to Peri play. Later two of the officers shut themselves up in one of the rooms of the house to discuss tactics. They are overheard to say that they will not allow the same thing to happen in Florence as had just happened in Rome. The people of the house make note of this, realising only in the light of subsequent events that it was a reference to the British promise to allow the Germans to retreat peacefully, and their breaking of this promise by firing on the retreating troops. (This, at least, is Barney's version of events). In the morning the Germans leave and the British take over the house ("these Anglo-Saxons with their well-shaped heads and small gentlemanly ears." [p. 245]) Once again the women go and soothe their highstrung nerves with Peri's delightful Bach recital. This time the British officers are invited. It could have been written by Guy de Maupassant. The bombing is fearful, and as Peri and her father gaze out of the windows toward Florence, they fly suddenly into tears of rage: the Germans are blowing up the famous Florentine bridges, one after the other (save the Ponte Vecchio).

Barney stood and watched the bombs, the flames, the smoke and that's How It Changed. It is impossible for her to deny the sight before her eyes: the champions of Art, History and Tradition are systematically destroying irreplaceable objects of beauty. It might be nice to think her mind was changed when she realised the fascists were systematically destroying irreplaceable human lives, but that's not what happened. Her reaction suggests she could not quite believe the Germans knew what they were doing:

> Could they not realise that the blowing-up of Florence's bridges would have a world-wide repercussion and make even the most cool-headed doubt the sanity of the whole totalitarian system? [p. 235]

A serious, fearful note surfaces here and there in the Memoirs despite the facade of "the jokes must go on." The Barney of the early 20th century who complained fretfully when everyone abandoned their tennis tournament to go and listen to the Dreyfus trial in Rennes [p. 169] has become more complex. The 1940s Barney confesses to undergoing what she terms a "sentimental crisis" (for which her friends recommend she read *Candide*) [p. 101]. She wonders,

Most certainly Romaine had the right to remain in Italy, but
had I? I had the uncomfortable impression of being towed in
her wake. [p. 50]

She describes herself,

I who may have no life ahead but only behind me... [p. 169]

This uneasiness builds up throughout the manuscript and one
begins to wonder whether her anti-semitism was the confused
product of more personal feelings. There is evident sexual jealousy
in some of her slights and insults. She demands, for example, by
what quirk of fate or intrigue Renée Vivien had come to leave her
for the arms of the "richest woman in the Israelite world?" [Barney
1960: 76]. She is outraged by the "Israelites" who, like Maurice de
Rothschild, handle society women as though they were mere
bibleots for their private collection. Maurice de Rothschild just
happened to be the protector of Liane de Pougy, another of Barney's lovers.

During the war, jealousy is a minor issue compared with that
of personal safety. Berthe Cleyrergue, Barney's housekeeper,
remained in Paris to look after Barney's house in the Rue Jacob.
She relates how in 1942 everything belonging to the Bertheims,
the Jewish owners of Barney's home, was sold by the Germans to
the Gauthier-Languereau publishing house. One day Cleyrergue
herself was summoned before the Germans who insisted that Barney was Jewish, intending to seize and sell her property as well.
Cleyrergue thought fast and replied that Barney was not Jewish,
certainly not, otherwise she never would have sought refuge with
Mussolini, now would she? And to respond to the vague rumours
the German officers had evidently heard about Barney's family,
Cleyrergue continued that they must be thinking of Barney's sister, Laura, who had indeed married a Jew, a Mr. Dreyfus, now
deceased. If they wished to interview Mrs. Dreyfus Barney, they
would find her in America. [Cleyrergue 1980: 148-151 and personal conversation of 26 July, 1991]. Had the Germans found
Natalie Barney at the house in 20 Rue Jacob, what would they

have done? By 1943 they were deporting people who had any Jewish relatives—Barney's own situation.

Was Barney aware of this situation? A paragraph in one of her letters to her sister is very revealing:

> Your post card on a photograph of St John's Church also reassured me that you are doubly safe under the care of both Church and State. Your sending this token was either a coincidence or a discreet response to my request for some documents avowing me "Arian"—and even a Christian (as my attitude suggests) and an Episcopalian as well, though whatever that may be I am no longer aware. [Barney MS: 31]

Barney needed proof that she was a Christian Aryan. Can this be that same woman who had to ask Renée Vivien, a few days before Christmas in the early 1900s, "What is this Christmas celebration? Does it commemorate the birth or death of Christ?" [Barney 1960: 55]. No wonder she has forgotten what Episcopalian means. Is the anti-semitism which fills the pages of the Memoir intended to express the Christian attitude to which she alludes in her letter to Laura?

Whereas in her earlier works she is quite open about her Jewish ancestry and proud of her family's achievements, by the time of "Memoirs" Barney has become extremely reticent. She writes of her father of "exclusively Anglo-Celtic stock," adding that her mother's ancestry is more varied: Her grandfather coming from Holland and her grandmother from France...[Barney MS: 126] There is a marginal note and a large question mark to the word "grandfather" saying "partly Jewish descent?" As though at the time of writing she cannot decide whether it is safe enough to admit to any degree of Jewishness but still does not like to deny it altogether. She explains her brother-in-law, with the obviously Jewish name "Dreyfus" as follows:

> My sister married a Frenchman interested like her in Eastern religions. [Barney MS: 96]

She writes of the Jews who subsidised the Grand Operas and

Philharmonic Orchestras—like Samuel Pike in Cincinnati and later New York—in terms that sound like praise, then ends her sentence with an aside about their hidden ambition to infiltrate high society. Her ambivalence becomes extremely apparent. She suggests that given the number of Jews who have been permitted to flood the USA, the name "Uncle Sam" should be changed to "Uncle Samuel." "Uncle Samuel?" "Granpa Samuel?"

What conclusion to draw? Is Barney allowed to remain a heroine? She laments that, unlike her ancestors who fled the French Revolution, she did not get the chance to be tested in some great feat of bravery:

> I wish I had been born in those troubled times, which demanded absolute heroism or total cowardice...
> [Barney 1910: 68]

It would seem that one must sigh and shake one's head, and say that she had indeed been so tested and that she failed.

But, leaving aside for a moment her written words, was there not during her four year stay in Fiesole, a moment when people turned to her for help, appealed to her to use her privileged position to keep them alive? There was. She and Romaine were at the Berenson's one day, watching Nijinsky's daughter dance, accompanied on the piano by a handsome young couple. Barney was attracted by handsome faces. At the end of the performance Mary Berenson drew Barney aside and asked,

> Where would this Jewish couple of musicians be able to take refuge that their child might be born in peace? ...I answered that they could have the cabin I had reserved on the "Rex" soon sailing for New York. [Barney MS: 26]

So, when it came to it, Barney replied without hesitation, without pomp and theory, a resounding "yes." I was so moved when I read this in the Bibliothèque Doucet that I wanted to cheer. I had so much wanted Barney to come out right in the end. Barney then wrote her sister, who was to have sailed with her, letting her know of the change she had made, so that Laura would not be startled and give the game away. Next, knowing that it was likely only Americans would be allowed to board this last boat from Genoa, she changed the names herself at Cooks Travel Agency, where the tickets had been purchased.

Well, so what? Why not give the tickets away, since she wasn't going to use them? And anyway, sounds like she gave that couple the tickets because they were good looking and played the piano so nicely. Did she? I don't know. I am more moved by acts of goodness than by vileness, probably because at that time they were so much more rare.

References

Barney, N.,   1910, *Eparpillements*, Paris Sansot
1918, *Pensées d'une amazone,* Paris Emile-Paul
1960, *Souvenirs indiscrets*, Paris Flammarion
1963, *Traits et portraits*, Paris, Flammarion
1963, *Traits et portraits*, Paris, Mercure de France
MS, *Memoirs of a European American* 1940-44

Benstock S., 1986, *Women of the Left Bank*, Austin, University of Texas Press
Cleyrergue B., 1980, *Berthe ou un demi-siècle auprè de l'amazone,* Editions Tierce, Paris
Jay K., 1988, *The Amazon and the Page*, Indianapolis, Indiana University Press
Vida, V., 1978, *Our Right to Love*, New Jersey, Prentice-Hall

Apology .... extract from *Pensées d'une amazone*
Dedication ....extract from *Pensées d'une amazone*
Reneé Vivien .... from *Souvenirs indiscrets*
The Woman Who Lives WithMe..
Privately printed, English in the original
Confidences ....extract from *Cinq petits dialogues gracs*
Brute! ....extract from *Cinq petits dialogues gracs*
Courtesan.........................extract from *Cinq petits dialogues gracs*
The Unknown Woman.......extract from *Cinq petits dialogues gracs*
Breasts...................................extract from *Traits et portraits*
The Climbing Rose...........................extract from *Accident*
The Sitting Room ....extract from *Accident*
Misunderstanding ....extract from extract from *Traits et portraits*
Gide and the Others........................extract from *Traits et portraits*
Illicit Love Defended........................extract from *Traits et portraits*
Predestined for Free Choice ....extract from *Eparpillements*
Scatterings ....extract from *Eparpillements*
Little Mistresses.................................extract from *Eparpillements*
Their Lovers..extract from *Eparpillements*
Epigrams..extract from *Eparpillements*
Indescretions...................extract from *Souvenirs indiscrets*
Alcohol................................. extract from *Pensées d'une amazone*
The Gods.......................extract from *Pensées d'une amazone*
Old Age .... extract from *Pensées d'une amazone*
Theatre................................ extract from *Pensées d'une amazone.*
Literature.............................. extract from *Pensées d'une amazone*
Critical Sallies........................ extract from *Pensées d'une amazone*
Rémy de Gourmont ....from *Souvenirs indiscrets*
The Colette I Knew................................from *Souvenirs indiscrets*
Gertrude Stein...Preface to *As Fine As Melanctha*, English in the
original. Reprinted from *Adam: International Review29* No 299
(1962)
When Poets Meet.....from *Adam: International Review 29* No 299
(1962)

Primary Sources

Barney, Natalie Clifford. *[Quelques portraits-sonnets de femmes,]* Paris: Société d'éditions littéraires, 1900.

——— .[Tryphé]. *[Cinqs petits dialogue gracs (antithèses et parallèles)].* Paris: Plume, 1902.

——— . *Actes et entr'actes.* Paris: Sansot, 1910

——— . *Eparpillements.* Paris: Sansot, 1910.

——— . *Pensées d'une amazone.* Paris: Emile-Paul, 1920.

——— . *Poems et poèmes: autres alliances.* Paris: Emile-Paul; New York: Doran 1920

——— . *Aventures de l'esprit..* Paris, 1929; rpt. New York: Arno, 1975

——— . *The One Who Is Legion, Or A.D.'s After-Life.* London: Partridge, 1930.

——— . *Nouvelles pensées de l'amazone.* Paris: Mercure de France, 1939

——— . *Souvenirs indiscrets.* Paris: Flammarion, 1960.

——— ."Idleness." *Adam : International Review* 29, No 299 (1962) 49-53

——— ."My Country 'tis of Thee.", *Adam: International Review* 29, No. 299 (1962) 67-71.

——— . *Traits et portraits.* Paris, 1963; rpt. New York: Arno 1975.

——— . *Accident.* MS. Bibliothèque Doucet, Paris.

——— . *Aphorisms of an Amazon.* MS. Bibliothèque Doucet, Paris.

——— . *Autour d'une victoire.* MS. Bibliothèque Doucet, Paris.

——— . *Jews, Poets and Poets.* MS. Bibliothèque Doucet, Paris.

——— . *Memoirs of a European American.* MS. Bibliothèque Doucet, Paris.

——— . *My Country tis of Thee.* MS. Bibliotheque Doucet, Paris.

——— . *La question juive et la terre promise.* MS. Bibliothèque Doucet, Paris.

[Barney, Natalie Clifford]. *Je me souviens.* Paris. Sansot, 1910.

[Barney, Natalie Clifford]. *The Woman Who Lives With Me.* n.p.: privately printed, n.d.

Secondary Sources

Adam: International Review 29, No 299 *The Amazon of Letters, A World Tribute to Natalie Clifford Barney,* 1962 Ed Miron Grindea, London.

Benstock, Shari. *Women of the Left Bank.* Austin: University of Texas Press, 1986.

Causse, Michéle and Cleyrergue, Berthe. *Berthe ou un demisiècle auprès de l'amazone.* Paris: Editions Tierce, 1980

Chalon, Jean. *Portrait d'une séductrice.* Paris: Stock, 1976.

Chapon, François, et al. *Autour de Natalie Clifford Barney.* Paris: Universités de Paris, 1976.

Cleyrergue, Berthe. *Personal Interview.* 26 June 1991.

Colette. *The Vagabond.* New York: Farrar Straus and Young, 1955.

———. *The Pure and the Impure.* New York: Farrar Straus and Giroux, 1967

———. *The Evening Star: Recollections.* London:Peter Owen, 1973.

———. *Duo and Le Toutounier.* Indianapolis: Bobbs-Merrill, 1974.

———. *Looking Backwards.* Bloomington: Indiana University Press, 1975.

Gide, André. *The Immoralist.* New York: A. A. Knopf, 1954.

———. *Corydon.* New York: Farrar, Straus and Giroux, 1983.

Gourmont, Rémy de. *Letters to the Amazon.* London: Chatto and Windus, 1931.

———. *Lettres intimes à l'amazone.* Paris: La Centaine, 1927.

Gramont, Elisabeth de. Ex-duchesse de Clermont-Tonnerre. *Mémoires...* Paris: Grasset, 1928.

———. *Pomp and Circumstance.* New York: J. Cape and H. Smith, 1929.

———. *Years of Plenty.* New York: J. Cape and H. Smith, 1931.

———. *Mémoires de la Tour Eiffel.* Paris: Grasset, 1937.

———. *Barbey d'Aurévilly.* Paris: Grasset, 1946.

———. *Marcel Proust..* Paris: Flammarion, 1948.

Harris, Bertha. "The More Profound Nationality of Their Lesbianism: Lesbian Society in Pairs in the 1920's" *In Amazon Expedition: A Lesbian-feminist Anthology.* Ed. Phyllis Birkby et al. New

York: Times Change Press, 1973, pp 77-88.

—— ."Lesbian Literature: An Introduction." In *Our Right to Love*. Ed. Vida, Virginia. New Jersey: Prentice- Hall, 1978, pp 257-259.

Jay, Karla. *The Amazon and the Page*. Indianapolis: Indiana University Press, 1988.

——. *The Amazon was a Pacifist.. Reweaving the Web of Life: Feminism and Nonviolence*. Ed. Pam McAllister. Philadelphia: New Society, 1982.

Loüys, Pierre. *Aphrodite*. Paris: A. Michel, 1946.

——. *Les Chansons de Bilitis*. Paris: Jobert, 1971.

Pougy, Liane de. *Idylle Saphique*. Paris: Plume, 1901

Vivien, Renée. *Brumes des fjords*. Paris: Lemerre, 1902.

——. *Une femme m'apparut...* 1904; rpt. Paris: Desforges, 1977.

——. *Poèmes en prose*. Paris: Sansot, 1909.

——. *Poèmes de Renée Vivien*. 2 vols. Paris, 1923; rpt. New York: Arno, 1975.

[Vivien, Renée, trans.]*Sapho*. Paris: Lemerre, 1909.

Wickes, G., *The Amazon of Letters: The Life and Loves of Natalie Barney*, New York: Putnam's, 1976.